The Psyche as Sacrament

Marie-Louise von Franz, Honorary Patron

**Studies in Jungian Psychology
by Jungian Analysts**

Daryl Sharp, General Editor

The Psyche as Sacrament

A Comparative Study
of
C.G. Jung and Paul Tillich

John P. Dourley

For Mary Briner and Ian Baker

Canadian Cataloguing in Publication Data

Dourley, John P., 1936-
   C.G. Jung and Paul Tillich

(Studies in Jungian psychology; 7)
Includes index.

ISBN 0-919123-06-6

1. Jung, C. G. (Carl Gustav), 1875-1961.
2. Tillich, Paul, 1886-1965.   3. Psychoanalysis and
religion.   I. Title.   II. Series.

BF51.D68   200.19   C81-094708-0

INNER CITY BOOKS
Box 1271, Station Q, Toronto, Canada M4T 2P4

Honorary Patron: Marie-Louise von Franz.
Publisher and General Editor: Daryl Sharp.
Editorial Board: Fraser Boa, Daryl Sharp, Marion Woodman.

INNER CITY BOOKS was founded in 1980 to promote the understanding and practical application of the work of C.G. Jung.

Cover: Medieval representation of the Christian quaternity,
   showing the Virgin Mary (the feminine principle) as the completion
   of the Trinity (Basil Museum; French School, 1457).

Back Cover Photos: C.G. Jung by Karsh of Ottawa, Paul
   Tillich by Archie Lieberman.

Index and Glossary by Daryl Sharp.

Printed and bound in Canada by Webcom Limited.

CONTENTS

See final pages for details of other

The glorification of the body portrayed as the coronation of the
Virgin Mary. The scene represents the alchemical quaternity: Father, Son, and Holy Spirit (dove), with the feminine (matter) as
the fourth (see text, pages 55ff).—*Rosarium Philosophorum*, 1550.
Psychological wholeness is universally symbolized by such four-
fold structures, often in circular or mandala form, as depicted on
the cover.

1 The Apologetic Problem

Carl Jung and Paul Tillich could well be hailed as two of the greatest apologists for Christianity the twentieth century has produced. They could equally well be dismissed as two of its greatest heretics. Tillich has described himself as *christianis paganus,* "to the Christians a pagan," a succinct statement of one side of the Christian community's response to him and to his theology. Similarly, Jung's conflicts with theologians are legendary. They fill many pages of the two volumes of his collected letters and are never far from the surface in his extensive writings on the psychology of religion.

Jung's rejection by large segments of orthodoxy during his lifetime was a source of continuing pain and bafflement to him.[1] Like Tillich he understood his work to be in the defence and service of the religious nature of man, a nature he sought to portray as a wealthy source of living symbols including the Christian ones. He hoped to provide the Christian with a deeper appreciation of his own symbols by demonstrating their source in the deeper reaches of the psyche. By thus showing the believer his continuity with the universal expressions of the human spirit both prior to and beyond Christianity, Jung sought to give new life and relevance to what had often become dead dogma. And yet his views were widely offensive to the collective Christian consciousness.

At the heart of the ambivalent reactions to these two men lies a paradox common to the thought of both. Jung and Tillich affirm that the reality of religion is embedded in the fabric of the human soul, and that it finds inevitable expression in the consciousness that arises from such depths. As such, religion cannot be eradicated from the human condition. Both men, with little variation, contend that the reality of religion, when it loses its specifically religious trappings, reappears in the guise of political, social, or philosophical and cultural notions, or indeed in anything to which can be appended the suffix "ism."

But combined with their unwavering sense of the inescapability of the religious factor in personal and social life was their equally clear perception of the ambiguous nature of religion itself, and their shared conviction that it could kill as well as enliven, split as well as heal, and fragment as well as make whole. In their eyes man was not faced with the choice of being religious or irreligious. His only real option was his free and responsible facing and coming to terms with the religion-engendering forces within his life. These forces might appear as obviously religious or they might appear in the compelling attractions of the apparently nonreligious dimensions of life. But appear they would and with the force of the suprahuman, with the force of the gods. The only real question, then, was not whether man would be approached by the divine in life but whether his response to its approach would destroy or support him. One of the lasting challenges from Tillich and Jung to the religionist, theologian, and believer is thus the task of elaborating a norm which might function to differentiate the destructive from the creative within the religions. This challenge would in effect put once more to the modern mind the ancient question, "Is there protection from the gods and if so wherein does it lie?"

In a preliminary manner it may be said that both Tillich and Jung answer this question by saying that if the gods are to be dealt with they must first be recognized as those powers within life greater than our conscious resources, powers which demand dialogue with ego consciousness. These powers seek to balance and to expand the ego, a divine invitation to growth which the ego refuses only with great danger to itself. For the gods man meets in himself are as demanding as any of the more traditional portraits of the God whose wrath descends from heaven, and, in the final analysis, are as ultimately benign. The difference, when seen from within, is that God's demand and consolation become part of one's immediate experience and not a response to a revelation which has occurred in another life.

In their biographical reflections and in their major works, Jung and Tillich show an acute awareness of the destructive side of religion in general, and specifically of the religion into which they were born. Each in his own way entered into the apologetic task on behalf of a Western humanity whose religion had, in their estimate, turned against its own spiritual needs and whose culturally predominant myth and symbol system, Christianity, could no longer offer it sufficient spiritual sustenance. Their concern for the spiritual needs of their times led both men to call for a restoration of the sense and meaning of religion itself, and for a consciousness that could again appreciate and respond to the symbolic, the native language of religion, as the two major preconditions for the revitalization of religion in any of its positive manifestations including Christianity.

This sense of religion, they argued, could be restored only if man could regain his experience of himself as an image of God. This recovery for both Tillich and Jung meant a heightened experience of the immediate presence of God to human consciousness and being. Psychologically, for Jung, this meant the identification and recognition of those structures and forces within the psyche from which man's experience of God both could and has to arise. Theologically, for Tillich, this meant grounding the being and life of man so intimately in the being and life of God that man's depth perception of himself becomes the doorway to the experience, however ambiguous and fragmentary, of the divine as the ground of human being. Put more formally, both men suggest—and Tillich demands—that the experience of the deep recesses of the psyche within life is the basis of a humane perception of God beyond life. The sense of divine immanence is the basis for man's sense of a transcendent God.

Not only do Jung and Tillich agree that man's sense of the divine arises from within, they also lay the basis for a possible further accord on the content or substance of that experience of God. For both take the general position that the transcendent powers that operate through life from its depths act, however painfully, to balance and extend life and consciousness. Thus Tillich affirms that the *telos* of life, the direction along which it is naturally urged, is to an ever fuller participation in the balanced flow of the divine life in which the human is naturally grounded. Similarly, Jung argues that the *deus absconditus,* the God hidden in man's unconscious, becomes incarnate through human consciousness and in so doing revitalizes, balances, and enlarges life, even as the symbols of death and resurrection are most apt to describe the dynamics of this interaction.

In the debate between modern theologies that would deny a natural continuity between the divine and the human, and those that would base their conception of religious man upon such a continuity, Tillich and Jung clearly align themselves with the latter. To understand man's relation to God in any other way is to place God as a being wholly beyond man and to conceive of Him as addressing or entering human life wholly from beyond it. Such intrusive revelations are experienced by their recipients as emanating from a source foreign to life, and tend to split rather than heal the life and consciousness they invade. Tillich and Jung seek to heal this breach by proposing a dialectical unity between man's sense of himself as autonomous and God's approach to him as a power transcendent to his humanity but not discretely separable from it.

Lord Acton wrote of papal infallibility, "Power corrupts. Absolute power corrupts absolutely." Tillich and Jung might write, "God as other alienates. God as wholly other alienates wholly." The thought of both men is hostile to an absolute split between the divine and the human. Behind such a split is an imaginal pattern, if not an ontological assertion, that the only manner in which God can address man is by imposing on him from outside. Frequently such models involve a transcendent God who reveals to man abstruse if not nearly unintelligible dogmas, and binds him to moral and cultic demands that are equally impositional and divested of a human sense. The foreign element that attaches to such revealed creeds, codes, and cults appears too often as an affront to the human mind, will, and dignity. They breed, especially since the Enlightenment, a rejection as abrupt and severe as their imposition, with the loss of all relation to the religious or else a placid obedience in which the fully human is diminished. Such models divide man's allegiance between his humanity and his religious nature and drive him to assert one at the cost of the other. The split faces man with the choice of his humanity or of his religious nature. The wholly other God accepts no compromise.

Tillich is most aware of how this split and splitting model of God's relation to man can be put theologically. Basing the split between man and God on the split between the natural and supernatural is one of the most powerful presentations of this idea. In this model the supernatural, and particularly the reality of supernatural grace, are wholly extirpated from creation and humanity, and are conferred upon it from without by a wholly free and contingent act on the part of a transcendent God. This model not only splits the natural from the supernatural but also splits the function of God as redeemer from that of God as creator. Tillich wonders, in the face of this model, how God in a redemptive action could enter structures of mind and soul in man, structures he has authored in creation and from which he is wholly absent, without destroying them or coercing them in a manner hostile to man. Such a conception of the redeeming, gracing, or revealing God he calls demonic.[2] Jung, too, respects so greatly the integrity of man's psyche that he is driven to affirm, in a process of reasoning similar to Tillich's, that man could not be aware of God unless through his psyche. This belief presupposes that the structures giving rise to man's sense of God reside permanently within the psyche.[3] (These structures are what Jung called archetypes.)

In response to the splitting model of God's presence to man, Jung and Tillich proffer a theological anthropology and accompanying apology based on a dialectical unity and disunity between the divine and the human. This dialectic functions in such a way that the divine, present in human experience from the dawn of self-consciousness, leads man personally and collectively into ever fuller, more meaningful, and more widely related configurations of consciousness. From this perspective, any given state of consciousness is in principle always capable of being transcended as it assimilates ever more of the divine matrix which gave birth to it and drives it in its growth.

This process can be described as God within man leading him to ever wider horizons, or as uniting man's opposites and the warring elements of his humanity in richer, more balanced unities, for which the price is the repeated rhythm of the death of an older, more constricted consciousness, followed by a new life of extended awareness. Though described differently by Tillich and Jung, the main consideration in their model of God's presence to man is that of a power within life which moves it to increasing transcendence of itself, in patterns of expansion of concern and of consciousness, even as this life retains its inner unity.

The putting of a sense of man's immanental connectedness with God as the precondition of man's sense of a transcendent God may seem like a relatively obscure theological or philosophical point. But for Tillich and Jung it becomes crucial. It is the necessary presupposition in the development of a conception of man's relation to God wherein God fosters life from within life, rather than constricting life by imposing upon it from without. Such concerns give life to Jung's psychology of religion and to Tillich's massive *Systematic Theology.* Both aim at alleviating the spiritual suffering caused by the more constrictive models of man's relation to God.

In his autobiography, Jung, with great poignancy, relates how the religious convictions of his minister father gradually came to steal the joy from his father's life, and may have contributed to its premature ending. Early in life Jung perceived that his father's discussions of theological matters were divorced from any personal experience.[4] In particular his father's ideas about God lacked any appreciation of that dark, chthonic and yet creative side of God which the younger Carl caught in his early vision of the Deity defecating on the Basel cathedral. In these early relations with his father Jung first clearly discerned the barrier which exists between a theology based on a conception of belief or faith as a coldly willed assent to the revealed unintelligible, and his own later insistence on experiential awareness as the basis of belief in the most obscure aspects of the Christian mystery such as the Trinity.[5] And Jung's early experiences of his father's conception of faith as an act of the will may be the basis for his later repeated equation of belief with metaphysics, the implication being that neither have anything to do with human experience, empirical or otherwise. In *Aion,* for instance, Jung writes that modern Christian conceptions of dogma provide it with "no basis in any experience that would demonstrate its truth."[6]

This emphasis on experience also explains Jung's remark in later years in reply to a question on his belief in God. He replied that he did not believe but *knew*. This response was quite consistent with his earlier leaning towards the view that faith and experience were not opposites, or need not be, and that the latter should always ground the former. In this belief Jung is not far from Tillich's conception of faith as Christian gnosis which combines in itself elements of thought, assent, and affect in an *amor intellectualis*.[7] But this view of faith demands an intimacy in being between God and man, and ultimately what Tillich calls the point of coincidence or intersection between the two.[8] Out of this intimacy of shared being and life proceeds all of religious experience, which gives rise to revelation and its symbols. Thus the symbol, when fully responded to, leads the believer into the same experience of God which originally gave rise to the symbol.

According to Jung his father was immune to this experience, known early to Carl, where "nothing separated man from God."[9] This absence of an experiential dimension to his father's faith became evident to Carl early on in his preparation for confirmation. Reading ahead of his father's instructions, Jung had been fascinated by the mystery of the Trinity as somehow an affront to the dull and unconvincing rationalism that surrounded so much of the dogma.[10] This youthful fascination with the Trinity endured in Jung's life. He was later to see it as a symbol of the flow of energy in all self-conscious and self-renewing systems of life, both human and divine.[11] But, at the time, as the young Carl awaiting so eagerly his father's addressing the mystery, he was greatly disappointed when his father simply admitted that he did not understand it and instead recommended, by implication, an attitude of loyal incomprehension. In contrast to his father's experiential and affective distance from the content of his belief expressed so clearly in this incident, Jung writes that even as a youth, "God was, for me at least, one of the most certain and immediate of experiences."[12]

Consistent with this experience, Jung, from his earliest days, showed a puzzled attitude towards those who sought to "prove" the existence of God.[13] In his mature work Jung insists that man's innate sense of God was the object of a *consensus gentium* coextensive with the history of consciousness.[14] Like Tillich, and in words almost identical to his, Jung identifies this consensus with the substance of the ontological argument as it recurs in the history of Western theology and philosophy.[15]

Given the disparity between his view of religion as a source of immediate experience and life and the more collective view held by his father, it is not surprising that for a time in his youth Jung came to look upon the church as a place of death. "It is an absence of God," he writes. "It is not life that is there but death."[16] Moreover he came to see his father as a tragic figure separated from, rather than led into, the source of life by his belief. In Jung's evaluation, his father's lack of any serious personal experience of that in which he believed led inevitably to a doubt whose constant repression had a debilitating effect on his life. Jung writes of the impact of the Church on his father with a certain note of anger and sorrow. "They had blocked all avenues by which he might have reached God directly and then faithlessly abandoned him."[17] Religion cut off from its experiential basis in man became for Jung a demand that man "believe without hope."[18] In describing his father's state of mind in his declining years, Jung relates that his father's only happiness was found when he could regain the zest of his student days, a time when he "was what he should have been."[19]

In spite of this early experience, Jung came to see religion as potentially a life-enhancing force. He was deeply impressed by its continuous emergence in myriad forms throughout the history of the human spirit, and gradually he came to locate its generative source in the deepest levels of man's unconscious. Keenly aware of its inevitability and of both its creative and destructive power, Jung finally believed that the religious instinct, understood in its widest sense, offered to life its greatest fulfillment. Thus he could write that the improvement of his patients in the second half of life was invariably accompanied by the recovery of a religious sense.[20]

This development in Jung's thought on religion was due to his realization that the possibility of the experience of the numinous, and so the possibility of religious experience, was grounded in the activation of archetypal forces in the psyche itself. Generally speaking, these forces acted to compensate, expand, and direct the ego towards what he came to call the self, the archetype of wholeness and the regulating centre of the personality. The experience of the reality of the self emerges from the growing conjunction of the ego and the unconscious in the process Jung terms individuation, which is itself both the direction in which life moves and its goal.

Tillich's theology, and the apology it contains, reveals as one of its own central concerns the paradox of the inevitability of a religious dimension in life which can be a power for life or death. Like Jung's, Tillich's understanding of the reality of religious experience and of faith is profoundly experiential and immediate. His controlling image of faith and of the universal religiosity of man which it presupposes is that of "ultimate concern." He means by this that man is constitutionally and inescapably concerned with the ultimate and, therefore, dialectically at one with it, however widely disparate an expression or object this concern be given. Tillich believes, indeed, that men not ultimately concerned, however they define their concern, are less than fully human. In other words, faith as ultimate concern is for Tillich universal, much in the manner that Jung attributes a certain universality, at least as a human potential, to the experience of the numinous as it rises from the unconscious to engage the ego. And, like Jung, Tillich refers to the ambiguity which surrounds man's religious capacity. "Our ultimate concern can destroy us as it can heal us," he writes. "But we never can be without it."[21]

For Tillich the destructive side of belief is its idolatrous potential. For this reason, in Tillich's hierarchy of sin as self-destruction idolatry ranks very highly. It constitutes an attack on the process of growth and so on life itself. It does this because Tillich's understanding of faith as ultimate concern presupposes that, though man and his mind participate immediately in the being of the ultimate as the precondition of his search for it, neither man nor his creations, nor anything finite, can ever be identified with it. For man to invest himself in the less than ultimate, or to define himself wholly with the penultimate or the finite, however sublime, is to deny his nature as belonging to the ultimate, as separated from it and yet as driven to regain it. Thus the true evil of idolatry for Tillich is to give oneself to the less than ultimate.

To make this point Tillich often uses examples of the pursuit of power and fame, or national and political ideologies. Whatever comes between man and the ultimate, which draws him on from within, functions as a false god to which man religiously devotes himself and by which he is ultimately betrayed because it lacks the capacity to answer his deepest needs and aspirations. This is the process Tillich has in mind when he writes that idolatrous faith "leads to a loss of the centre and to a disruption of the personality."[22]

Like Tillich, Jung too sees the dynamics of human life given to the inevitable production of many gods. Man may locate the ultimate in various realities but seems to have little choice about locating such a reality. Jung writes on this point:

> In the language of analytical psychology . . . the actual God-concept is, psychologically, completely different in different people, as experience testifies. . . . For, as we know, the highest value operative in a human soul is variously located. There are men "whose God is in the belly" (Phil. 3:19), and others for whom God is money, science, power, sex, etc. The whole psychology of the individual, at least in its essential aspects, varies according to the localization of the highest good, so

that a psychological theory based exclusively on one fundamental instinct, such as power or sex, can explain no more than secondary features when applied to an individual with a different orientation.[23]

Tillich's religious-psychological analysis of the dynamics of the human life process is unintelligible unless it be presupposed that the being of God is dialectically at one with the being of man. He describes this divine reality as preserving man from self-destruction by uniting harmoniously the opposites that make up his humanity, and in so doing moving every life to the fullest balanced growth it can bear. For Tillich it is precisely the healing unification and onward leading activity of God *within* man that grounds and makes possible the experience of God *beyond* man.

Tillich occasionally puts this point in dramatic ways. In one of his most famous essays he proposes two models of an understanding of God which, he suggests, exhaust the theological possibilities of how God's presence to man may be understood. Each model has its own discernible psychological position.[24] On one hand God is met as a stranger whose meeting occasions further estrangement of man from himself, his fellows, and nature. On the other hand God is met as a power from which man has become estranged, which implies a previous unity now diminished but never wholly broken. This continuity between God and man serves as the basis of both the possibility and necessity of communion between God and man. By it man is driven to recover his essential humanity expressed eternally in God, a humanity from which he is fallen in time but from which he is never fully severed. This inherence in the divine is the universal human situation for Tillich. The intensification of man's experience of this reality relates man more wholly to himself, to his fellow man, and to nature, since through it he intersects within himself the power that gives rise to all. Tillich sees much of the substance of Western theology centred on the issue of these competing models of God's presence to man.

The second model sees the being of man as never wholly separated from its divine matrix, even in the distortions, splits, and fragmentation of existence. This continuity grounds man's universal experience of God and his ultimate concern. In this view the power of God works through the depths of life to lead man to his higher or essential humanity as expressed in God. The first view sees God as discontinuous with man, whom he first creates, and, on the occasion of his contingent fall, arbitrarily redeems. In this model God relates to creation and to man externally and causally. He brings creation into existence, holds it in existence, and intervenes in it from time to time in a manner which might be described as both casual (because non-necessary) and intrusive (because from beyond). It is this externalization, with its split between the natural and the supernatural, between the word of God and the word of man, with its accompanying contingency and arbitrariness and with its expulsion of God from the fabric of being, both human and natural, that Tillich spent much of his theological energies combatting.

To this model of God's presence to man he hoped his work would offer a humane alternative. At the centre of his theological anthropology is his repeated assertion that once the enlivening dialectical unity between the being of God and the being of man has been cut, so is lost the possibility of religion as a humanizing force. Once the religious dimension of life becomes a superaddition, it loses its ultimacy and breeds its own rejection. For Tillich, if serious atheism is made possible by a conception of man from which the experience of God is removed as an immediate and universal possibility, then atheism soon becomes a necessity. Indeed, Tillich sees the inevitable secularization and atheistic affirmation in the West as stemming from St. Thomas Aquinas' conception of religious man.[25]

Arguing the same point from a slightly different perspective, closer now to the psychological, Tillich contends that unless the genesis of faith derives from the depths of man's being it cannot touch man in his wholeness, and so easily becomes unwholesome. Faith then excludes a part of man. Much like Jung in his discussiion of the shadow, Tillich argues that the excluded part of man will rebel against whatever faculty is endowed with the privilege of being the seat of faith, just as the privileged faculty must repress the rest in the maintenance of its favoured position. Such faith, far from healing, divides man within himself by pitting part against part in inner warfare.

*

In his work devoted to the nature of faith, Tillich reveals his indebtedness to the insights of what he calls "analytic psychology."[26] In his view this psychology describes the dynamic of personal life in terms of polarities in interaction, and he contends that the dynamics of faith must be as all-embracing as the dynamics of personality. "The first and decisive polarity in analytic psychology," he writes, "is that between the so-called unconscious and the conscious."[27] In accord with his holistic view of faith he adds, "Faith as an act of the total personality is not imaginable without the participation of the unconscious elements in the personality structure."[28] Here Tillich shows an awareness much like Jung's, namely that if the reality and power of the unconscious are denied by consciousness, then the unconscious, autonomous forces (or complexes) invariably limit the available energy and so the ego's freedom of thought and action. Tillich thus understands freedom to be closely related to healthy faith, in that both are incompatible with unconscious compulsion.

Again, in terms reminiscent of aspects of Jung's thought, Tillich too introduces a conception of the self into his treatise on faith. He refuses to reduce the reality of faith to any exclusive aspect of consciousness or willfulness on one hand, or to the prerational or irrational on the other. For these reasons, when Tillich defines faith in a negative manner by showing what it is not, he denies that it is a power which can be located in the intellect, the will, or the affections alone.[29] Nor is it to be understood as a process in which one of these faculties moves the others against their native propensities, as in Aquinas' understanding of the will moving the intellect to assent to truths beyond the pale of evidence. Rather Tillich locates faith in an act combining but transcending all of these faculties. "Faith is not an act of any of [man's] rational functions," he writes, "as it is not an act of the unconscious, but it is an act in which both the rational and nonrational elements of his being are transcended."[30] The subject of this act of faith, which seems at the same time to be a resultant of it, is what Tillich calls, "[man's] self, the center of self-relatedness in which all elements of his being are united."[31]

Both Tillich and Jung understand the self to be that centering force within the psyche which brings together the opposites or polarities, whose dynamic interplay makes up life itself. For Jung the greatest of these polarities are consciousness and the unconscious. The nature of these polarities, when functioning in creative reciprocity, is to produce a centre of the personality, a self, which is neither the ego nor the unconscious but the product of their marriage or union. From one perspective the self, for Jung, precedes the unity of ego and unconscious and works to bring it about. From another perspective it is the resultant of the unity of ego and unconscious. In this sense it exists from the outset of life but is only achieved, and then only approximately, at the end of the process.

Tillich's conception of the self also implies that if a man's faith is to be as encompassing as man is, it must include the reality of the unconscious. To conceive of faith in lesser terms is to exclude from it an immense portion of man's totality. Indeed, the unconscious may make it painfully evident to those with a limited conception of faith that their faith is not large enough to accommodate the full sweep of their humanity. Perhaps it was just this which Jung saw as so constricting his father's life.

As Jung locates within life the reality of the unconscious, "which is of indefinite extent with no assignable limits,"[32] so does Tillich locate the infinite within man. On these grounds both point to the universal possibility and general necessity of man's experience within life of that which transcends his consciousness, and, by implication, his finitude itself. In lines that resonate with the spirit of Jung, Tillich writes:

> Man's experiences, feelings, thoughts are conditioned and finite. They not only come and go, but their content is of finite and conditional concern—unless they are elevated to unconditional validity. But this presupposes the general possibility of doing so; it presupposes the element of infinity in man. . . . This alone makes faith a human potentiality.[33]

In terms of his overall thought it is fair to state that Tillich equates the experience and reality of the infinite with the experience and reality of God. For him to say that the presence of "an element of the infinite in man" makes faith possible, is the equivalent of saying that man's sense of God is made possible by the presence of God in man's being and consciousness. Tillich means this in a strict ontological and epistemological sense. Put simply, Tillich takes the position that the possibility of man's awareness of God derives from the fact that man participates in the being of God. Consciousness of this participation is consciousness of that reality men have traditionally called God, and also the basis in life of what Tillich calls man's ultimate concern. In effect, then, Tillich performs from a theological perspective the same task Jung performs from a psychological one, when Jung points to the genesis of all religious experience in an experience of the numinous, grounded in the impact of the collective unconscious on the ego.

Each seems to be here describing the dynamics of the imprint of the divine on the human. If anything, the psychologist, Jung, shows greater restraint than the theologian, Tillich. For Jung, in his more measured treatment of the origin of the numinous, points only as far as the apparently inexhaustible capacity of the unconscious to throw up discernibly similar images of God on a consistent and universal basis. Jung grounds this capacity in the archetypes of the collective unconscious. In so doing he confines himself to the phenomenological and empirical evidence derived from patterns of images that point to a common (i.e., archetypal) origin. He absolves himself from speculation on the actual existence of God, though in less guarded moments he hints that the archetypes themselves may penetrate to "the very ground of the universe."[34] Tillich, the ontologist and epistemologist, goes beyond Jung in this respect, taking the firm position that man's sense of God is made possible only because man's being is grounded in God's. Thus the presupposition of man's search for God is his always ambiguous possession of and by Him.[35]

This dialectical intimacy of God and man is at the centre of Tillich's theological methodology, which he calls the method of correlation and which he understands as the basis for his theology as an "answering" theology.[36] It presupposes man's ambivalent experience of a simultaneous unity with and separation from his divine ground. The very dynamic of this experience both draws man back to his source and yet convinces him that he cannot reachieve wholeness unless it be given. Tillich captures the movements of this dynamic succinctly when he writes, "Man is the question he asks about himself before any question has been formulated."[37] Thus man, by the very nature of his existential situation, asks after God. Tillich believes that the experienced answer to this quest is the substance of the Christian revelation and the meaning of Christ. In the light of this understanding of the human situation, the task of the theologian is to analyse the ongoing and culturally variable expressions of the human plight and quest, and to address the resources of the Christian message to it.

Certain aspects of this methodology and the system Tillich builds on it are worthy of comment. First, Tillich presupposes man is driven to ask the question of God because of his experience of his dialectical unity with and distance from God. The underlying unity with God is the point in Tillich's system which separates him irreconcilably and irrevocably from Karl Barth and Kierkegaard, both of whom deny this point of coincidence between man and God. In this Tillich's sensitivities again show an affinity with Jung's. For Jung also distanced himself from Barth and Kierkegaard and largely over the issue of how and where the ultimate appeared in life.[38] Second, though Tillich demands of the theologian that he analyse the human situation, he maintains nevertheless that the answer comes from beyond. He writes, "God is the answer to the question implied in human finitude. This answer cannot be derived from the analysis of existence."[39] Further on this point he writes, "But revelation is 'spoken' to man, not by man to himself."[40] In these passages Tillich is very concerned to show that the analysis of existence does not and cannot produce the answer to its problem. Otherwise he would be forced to admit that man could on his own efforts author his own salvation.

But, third, Tillich does imply that the answer to man's existential separation from his source can only rise to meet man's quest from and through the depths of his own being. Describing how man's search for the ultimate moves from outer to inner (and in so doing retracing the footsteps of Augustine in the *Confessions*), Tillich writes, "And then [man] has become aware of the fact that he himself is the door to the deeper levels of reality, that in his own existence he has the only possible approach to existence itself."[41] In a footnote he adds that he sees this position as having its predecessors in Augustine, Paracelsus, Boehme, and Schelling among others, all of whom affirm "the mystical identification of the ground of being with the ground of self."

Tillich here affirms that God is the ground of the self and that in the depths of his interiority man discovers the experience and reality of God. This would not deny Tillich's continued concern to show that revelation is spoken to man and not by man to himself. Rather it is to affirm that man is addressed by Another in his own interiority. Thus understood, the revelatory answer to man's existential plight could be quite easily conceived, in Tillichian terms, as mediated to the ego through the unconscious as the vehicle which connects man with the ultimate. Such a model would preserve the distinction between human question and divine answer, and point to the possible function of the unconscious as an inner voice speaking to man from within, yet from a position and with an authority transcendent to the ego.

Tillich's method of correlation could itself be correlated with Jung's understanding of the archetypal basis of the experience of the numinous and of revelation in the unconscious. It is also in accord with Tillich's central concern, which is to avoid both an impositional model of revelation and also the other extreme of reducing human consciousness to the purely autonomous or secular.

With his method of correlation, Tillich can show how the answer of revelation arises to meet and heal man from within, rather than further burden his humanity as a foreign imposition, while at the same time locating its genesis at a level of man's being that defies his manipulation and control. This view runs throughout his system in his conception of *theonomy*. For Tillich, theonomy means that man's truest law is the law of God written in the depths of his being. By this he avoids the extremes of autonomy, wherein man would seek to become his own law at the comparatively superficial level of reason and consciousness, and of heteronomy, wherein man as creature would simply bow to the imposing power of God.

Allied to the positions Tillich takes on man as religious, on revelation, and on the method of correlation is his position on *kerygmatic* and *apologetic* theology. Again in this discussion arise his differences with Barth.[42] Kerygmatic theology centres on the proclamation of the message and does not demand a reflection on the nature of revelation itself nor on the conditions of receptivity in man. In contrast to this, apologetic theology (and especially Tillich's version of it) is built on the need to relate the message to the culture by showing how it answers the questions about man asked by his current culture, and how it might critically but responsibly address the implications about ultimacy that Tillich claims are inevitably expressed by every significant cultural expression.

Tillich, of course, does not deny the need for the preservation of the substance of the kerygma or message, but he is insistent on the key role of the apologist, who must face the challenge of mediating the kerygma to his times. In fact, Tillich attributes whatever cultural credibility modern Christianity enjoys to the major apologetic efforts of the last two centuries.[43] The father of such efforts and a man whose thought he is openly dependent upon in his own system, Friedrich Schleiermacher, was also much respected by Jung and is credited by Jung with the baptism of his grandfather.[44] As the modern founder of the effort to relate Christianity to *homo religiosus,* it is not surprising that Schleiermacher was the bête noire of the neo-orthodox movement as it took shape after World War I under the guiding inspiration of Barth.

Again, from the perspective of the tensions between apologetic and kerygmatic theologies, Jung and Tillich share a model of man as religious, generating his symbols from his own depths and then relating his symbols to his culture; in this process the symbols are asked for their resources in addressing culture and culture is renewed or criticized in relation to the symbols.

In the matter of apologetic theology, Jung himself makes certain important suggestions. He takes the position that the major dogmas of Christianity are themselves grounded in the fabric of the psyche, and that their latency in the psyche and their potential universal expression, as well as their actual expression outside of Christianity, could serve as a "natural theology."[45] Such a natural theology would function to bridge the gap between man's theological and psychological self-consciousness by showing that all religious symbols derive from the collective unconscious. One of Jung's more brilliant applications of this lay in showing the universal implications and expressions of the symbol of the Trinity.[46] In his work on the Trinity he points to the pre-Christian and extra-Christian manifestations of this belief, and relates its basic meaning to the flow of life energies between the poles of consciousness and the unconscious.

Tillich, too, understands the way the doctrine of the Trinity is handled in any theological system as a major indication of the degree of integration which exists in that system between the revealed and the basis of the revealed in the psyche. In specific reference to the extrinsicism, biblicism, and authoritarianism in Barth's theology, Tillich writes, "It could be said that in [Barth's] system [the Trinity] falls from heaven, the heaven of an unmediated biblical and ecclesiastical authority."[47] In a manner quite in keeping with Jung's belief that religious symbols are grounded in the psyche, Tillich shows that man is the possessor of a natural and latent Trinitarian experience. Tillich argues that this latency is present in man's ambivalent experience of God as a *mysterium tremendum et fascinosum.*[48] This experience itself is one of the two sides of God united in one life process. With Tillich these two aspects or faces or moments in the divine life are those of abyss, the overwhelming side of God, in interplay with the ongoing definition of this abyss in the Logos or revelatory and fascinating side of God.

There are further significant parallels in the thought of Jung and Tillich. Both affirm some type of dependence of God on man for His completion or expression in creation. Thus Tillich contends that God both knows and prays to Himself through human self-consciousness.[49] Furthermore he implies that man's perception of God can discern the diverse phases of the divine life in its beneficent and wrathful power:

> There is a mutual interdependence between "God for us" and "we for God." God's wrath and God's grace are not contrasts in the "heart" of God (Luther), in the depth of his being; but they are contrasts in the divine-human relationship.[50]

Here he implies that the difference in God as wrathful or beneficent is based upon man's perception of God. In an early work on the demonic, Tillich had contended that the demonic is in fact that chaotic abyss, the nothingness of pure power as potentiality, out of which all definition proceeds.[51] The very definition and so expression of this power, and the harmonious relating of it to its origin through Spirit, makes possible man's sense of the beneficence of God. The consequence is that man's experience of the demonic is his experience of the unchained, unexpressed, and so undifferentiated aspect of the Godhead itself. Thus God must first differentiate Himself within Himself as the precondition of His expression beyond Himself. For Tillich this is a description of the substance of the meaning of the flow of intra-Trinitarian life. It also grounds the movement of human life in the divine, where it achieves something of the balance of opposites that constitutes divine life.

Similarly, in Jung's work on Job God is presented as made up of opposites which are undifferentiated in their primal expression, and become differentiated through the sufferings of Job and in the incarnation of Christ.[52] In this process the Logos again is seen as the differentiation of divine ambivalence in its incarnation and opposition to the devil or antichrist. But with Jung this differentiation takes place in time and not within the Trinity as with Tillich.

The intimacy which Tillich and Jung establish between the divine and the human lead both to reject a conception of revelation as a heterogeneous body imposed on man from without. Tillich argues that just such an image of revelation lies behind kerygmatic theology, and writes that in fact such a theology throws the message at men "like a stone."[53] Jung too felt that a certain unbecoming stridency can creep into professions of faith in revelation when these realities are not grounded in life:

> In my practice I often had to give elementary school lessons in the history of religion in order to eliminate, for a start, the disgust and nausea people felt for religious matters who had dealt all their lives only with confession-mongers and preachers.[54]

Tillich deems the discontinuities between man and God, which ground such models of faith and revelation, to be attacks on man's intrinsically religious nature as a seeker after God, and so as a form of "self-deception."[55] Jung too sees such denials as forms of self-deception, since he grounds man's sense of God in man's own psyche.[56]

At this point another central paradox appears in the thought of both men. Not only do they feel that religion can act to energize or to depress life by relating it to, or severing it from, its depths, they also feel that in large part the modern religious tradition in the West has chosen the latter option by removing the divine from the depths of life. As a consequence, Christianity is no longer capable of meeting collective spiritual needs. This has happened in large part through the endorsement of conceptions of God as transcendent by both reformed and Catholic Christianity, which by putting God beyond life has weakened if not removed the sense of God working within life.

Both Tillich and Jung feel that the spiritual void left in the wake of the Christian abdication has been filled by widespread adherence to political ideologies, what Jung terms "politico-social delusional systems" functioning as religions.[57] Neither are impressed by the submersion of the individual in the collective, which such systems usually demand as the price of salvation. Both call for a rediscovery of the nature of religion itself, as the precondition for the revitalization of any particular religion, including Christianity. This in fact would mean the recognition of the individual soul and psyche as the place of access to the divine, and the source from which man's symbols and their attendant numinosity arise. Not only would such a self-understanding reinvest the symbols of any particular religion with new life and urgency, it would also relate the holders of any specific pattern of religious symbols more empathically to other symbolic expressions. Put simply, the multiplicity of faiths might cease to culminate in religious antipathy, if not actual warfare. Rather the faiths and major religions might come to see themselves as offering to each other a much needed complementarity.

Thus both Tillich and Jung point to the need for a recovery of the mystical tradition within Christianity, and both endorse those aspects of the Platonic Christian tradition that point to a presence of God within man. Moreover, Tillich understands one of the duties of apologetic theology to be the use of culturally current modes of thought to draw out the implications of the specifically Christian message. With this in mind he saw depth psychology as a gift to theology, for it threw new light on the soul.[58] It also provided a heightened sense of sin as the universal estrangement of man from his truest or essential self,[59] and dramatically revealed "the reality of the demonic in everyone."[60] In Tillich's opinion, depth psychology helped to break a constrictive moral perfectionism divested of both the highs and lows of life, a moralism which could induce a sense of crippling guilt in those less successful in meeting its demands.[61] Even as it attacked this kind of moralism the psychoanalytic tradition provided a new sense of grace based on self-acceptance and acceptance of the other.[62]

Tillich also describes depth psychology in terms of a spiritual discipline. He sees it as a modern expression of the monastic tradition of self-examination. He understands its attraction for the Protestant mind as springing from the same needs which previously had attracted so many to Zen Buddhism.[63] In certain passages he also recognizes that depth psychology fills in the Protestant world the vacuum left by the loss of confession. And when he delineates the effects of the Holy Spirit on life, Tillich points to heightened awareness and freedom, the same effects he sees in applied depth psychology. In other words, the analytical process could be a means of mediating the Spirit.

*

It would be wrong to create the impression that no tension exists between the ways Tillich and Jung understand man as religious, or the manner in which they understand the relation of psychology to theology. For instance Jung repeatedly disavows any metaphysical import in his psychology. Jung usually means by the term "metaphysical" a position or doctrine without any basis in human experience, so he often relates it to an inadequate model of belief. But if the term is taken to mean a mental discipline that deals with the nature of being, and especially with the nature of human being and human knowing, then one wonders if Jung's work itself is really without metaphysical import. Take his theory of the psyche, which holds that all human awareness moves through the psyche, so that nothing foreign to it could attain human consciousness. His understanding of the collective unconscious locates there those factors, or archetypes, which when activated invest man with his sense of the divine and of the numinous. His understanding of the movement of psychic life towards individuation, or towards the self as the marriage of conscious and unconscious, implies a teleology and a value system wherein wholeness or completion functions as goal. All of these positions could be described as metaphysical.

Jung's defensiveness is certainly understandable considering the opposition he encountered in his lifetime. On the one hand his position on the immanental origin of religion was and is intolerable to a major segment of the theological world, which much prefers an extraneous revelation and an extraneous God. On the other hand, his peers in the field of psychology might well charge him with dabbling in metaphysics, in order to undermine the scientific basis of his work. Against both Jung could defend himself by pointing, as he did, to the empirical and phenomenological evidence on which he based his model of the psyche.

The impression arises from time to time that Jung intuitively grasped that his thought included the challenging vision of a potential unification of the theological, philosophical, and psychological worlds, and that this challenge would be too great to those who wished to live their lives within only one world turned prison. For the further reaches of Jung's thought confront one with the question as to whether or not he believed he had uncovered the source of religious experience, and so of all the religions, within the psyche of man. This question leads to another: If Jung had met with a theological receptiveness such as Tillich's theology could afford, might he have been able to work out, in a more favourable climate, a theological anthropology or a conception of the religious nature of man? The same question might be asked in regard to the psychological criticisms bent on denying a religious function or component in the psyche. Had Jung not needed to defend himself from the criticisms of hostile theologians and psychologists, he might not have found himself in the rather paradoxical position of muting the evident spiritual, theological, and philosophical implications of his thought in the name of the rather constricted views of man presented by nineteenth-century science on one hand, and orthodox Christian theologies on the other.

Tillich himself recognized the deeper metaphysical, philosophical, and spiritual dimensions of Jung's discoveries. In a tribute paid to Jung's work on symbols at the time of Jung's death, Tillich gives to Jung's thought the status of an ontology because its depth and universality constitute a "doctrine of being."[64] Tillich describes Jung as one "who knows so much about the depths of the human soul,"[65] by which he means a man naturally and deeply sensitive to the spirit. Jung himself might wince at his thought being described as a "doctrine" of anything, let alone being. But Tillich's point is that Jung deals consistently and, in the evolution of his model of the psyche, systematically, with "the mystery of the creative ground of everything that is."[66] To do so, for Tillich, is to enter into the realm of metaphysics because it is an attempt to identify those structures in the depths of man that universally determine his human nature, thinking, and response to the world.

If Jung qualified or denied the metaphysical import of his thought, Tillich qualified the relationship of the theological world to the psychological. In his *Systematic Theology,* where he characteristically expresses gratitude to depth psychology for what it has given or could give theology, he states also that the Christian owes allegiance to neither Freud nor Jung as possessing "revealed" psychologies.[67] Here his statements are determined by his concern to free religion and revelation, understood as deriving from man's relation to the ultimate, from any unqualified commitment to one position in the field of the humanities or of science. Rather Tillich understands the various positions in the humanities and the arts as each possessing and expressing some aspect of ultimacy.

On the other hand, while paying many tributes to Jung's psychology he seems, in certain passages, to express a deeper appreciation of Freud's. Hence he can describe Jung as a man who "knows so much about the depths of the human soul and about religious symbols, [who] thinks that there are essential structures in the human soul,"[68] but then go on almost immediately to point to a greater depth in Freud: "In all these representatives of contemporary depth psychology (including Jung) we miss the feeling for the irrational element that we have in Freud and in much of the existentialist literature."[69]

This apparent preference for Freud is strange both in the context of the article in which it appears and in the wider context of Tillich's thought itself. Here he seems to question Jung's search for "essential structures of the soul" as the basis of personality. Yet Tillich himself bases his understanding of religious man on a conception of essential humanity grounded in the Logos within Trinitarian life, a life in which man participates by nature and towards which he moves in the process of his humanization. Consistent with this side of his thought, Tillich goes on to criticize Freud for limiting himself to a consideration of existential man and divesting himself of a referent to essential man. For Tillich this amounts to removing from man the possibility of regaining his humanity and so his health. Tillich goes on to say that Freud involved himself here in a contradiction because he believed in "the healing process," even though his thought could not take him beyond a conception of man rooted irremediably in his "existential self-estrangement."[70]

Had Tillich been more consistent in his overall systematic viewpoint, he would have been forced to admit that Jung's psychology is far more capable of bearing his own conception of man as essentially related to the ultimate in his depths, separated from it in his existence, yet driven towards it as the healing source of his life. Perhaps it was not till Jung's death that Tillich realized this when he frankly acknowledged the theological importance of Jung's work on symbols.

Thus tensions do exist between the thought of Jung and Tillich, but the correspondences remain striking and deeper than the tensions. These links could be of great importance in the deepening and revitalizing of both psychology and theology, by showing to practitioners of each discipline the points of interconnection. However, this would necessarily involve the acceptance of certain positions and viewpoints that may remain irritants to theologian and psychologist for yet some time. These irritants and challenges centre around the following points. Both men are profoundly aware of the interpenetration of the psychological and religious dimensions of life. Jung understands the psyche as generative of the religious experience. Tillich in his theology of revelation and symbol formation sees a close connection between reason and its depths, and intimately relates the depth of reason with the reality of the divine.[71] Thus God for Tillich approaches consciousness from its depths, and consciousness is capable of capturing the experience of such an approach only in the symbol.

In line with this common insight, both Tillich and Jung understand the force of religion within life as working to unify the opposites that make up the dynamic substance of life, and so to lead life into patterns of balance and growth. This model of God's presence to life necessitates a close relation between the religious, spiritual, and psychological dimensions of man. In fact Tillich and Jung so closely interrelate these dimensions of man that, though they may be distinguishable, they are virtually inseparable, hence any inadequacy in one area shows up in the others. Consequently a theology that dismissed the psychological (on whatever grounds—pure humanism and reductive naturalism are two of the favourites), or a psychology which did not reach the psyche in its depths, where it functions as the matrix of meaning and spirituality, would be equally pathogenic. Any religious experience or theology or spirituality which presented itself as supernaturally acceptable, though humanly pathological, would be ruled out in principle. Neurosis in any form could not be a higher spirituality. Equally unacceptable would be the happy dissociation which practitioners of either psychology or theology might draw between their disciplines. For either to deny the challenge of the other would constitute a flight from the question of where *theos* and psyche might touch or indeed be, with all due nuances, one.

A further possible irritant, especially for the theological world, is found in the movement of their thought towards the universal and so towards relativity and tolerance. In this movement Jung is in the lead. Jung's view of the religions as grounded in universally possessed archetypes works to show that any particular historical manifestation (Christ, Buddha, Gandhi, etc.) never exhausts the possibilities of expression of the archetype that lies behind the manifestation. Given this model of the genesis of the religious experience, it is not possible to hold any given symbol system or revelation as exhaustive, absolute, or definitive.

Applying these principles to Christianity, Jung sees it of inestimable value and importance in the development of religious consciousness in the West. He describes Christianity and its symbols as a relatively adequate map of the unconscious. Indeed, though he documents its incompletion, he insists that it cannot be surpassed till it is lived through. (This is fully discussed in Chapter 6.)

On the question of the universalization and so relativity of symbols, Tillich's commitment to the symbol of Christ as the object of his ultimate concern makes his position somewhat more constricted than Jung's. But Tillich's Christology is a Logos Christology, and the Logos is itself both a universal principle and one which received formulation prior to Christianity. The obvious concern which moves Tillich to opt for a Logos Christology is his desire to show that the human Logos meets its essential inner-historical realization in the figure of Christ. Thus Tillich contends that the major dynamic which underlies and empowers all of man's religious quests is his sense of his own estrangement from his essential Logos and so from his essential humanity. For Tillich this was realized in the Christ.

Whatever be thought of this Christology, its obvious apologetic import is to show the universality of Christ by presenting the Christ event as the answer to man's universal, existential predicament, namely alienation from his essential being. Tillich is convinced that unless the historical Christ can be related to the fulfillment of a universal religious aspiration and expectation, then the human response to Christ can easily become idolatrous, leading to a personal hero worship that misses the depth of meaning of Christ and degenerates into what Tillich calls "Jesusology."[72]

Other points of correspondence which can both stimulate and irritate follow from their understanding of the intimacy of God's presence to man. It is difficult to escape the impression that some form of pantheism is endemic to the thought of each, and that this pantheism pushes easily to some form of monism. Tillich rejects a pantheism that would reduce God to nature by equating the two, as in Spinoza's formulation *"Deus sive natura."* He does however endorse a certain "panentheism," by which he alludes to the interpenetration of divine and created being, but in such a way that God's transcendence is preserved because it is more than the sum total of created being and its source and ground.[74] Jung, on his part, refers to the fact that Christianity has lost a sense of pantheism and, especially, a sense of God within the soul, a contributing factor in the soul's loss of spiritual power.[75]

Related to this is the question of God's completion through creation and human growth. Both Tillich and Jung endorse some understanding of God which would make creation necessary though non-compulsive, and which would visualize some form of divine self-completion in the emanation of creation from God. This is strongly implied in Tillich's image of man as existing in a state of "dreaming innocence" in the realm of divine essences, prior to his stepping out of the divine matrix into created existence through an act of will by which he actualizes himself.[76] In this dialectic, Tillich works to show creation and fall as two sides of the same process, but in so doing his thought demands that the eternal essences need to be expressed beyond God if they are to be real, even though their expression in creation is inevitably though freely related to their fall.

Here Tillich shows a certain affinity with Jung's insistence that the Trinity needs to complete itself through the missing fourth in the form of creation, matter, and even evil. Thus Jung speaks of a divine presence in matter, the *deus absconditus,* and contends that consciousness has the task of liberating "God" from his imprisonment in matter.[77] He seems to mean that the process of becoming more conscious is one in which man increasingly becomes aware of both his divine and demonic nature, a process of incarnation through differentiation. In some of his formulations Jung also implies that God becomes more conscious of Himself through man's growing self-consciousness, a view not so far from Hegel's insight, though Jung relates it to individual psychic growth while Hegel related it to growth in history.[78]

In this context Tillich and Jung also closely relate revelatory experience to self-discovery. Lest this lead to thoughts of an inflated identity of the human with the divine, both understand this self-discovery and growth to be, in principle, never completed and so always ambiguous within the confines of a personal and historical life process.

Certain central features in the thought of Tillich and Jung encourage a reexamination of the traditional distinctions between the natural and the supernatural. Tillich is explicit in working to overcome the split. In doing so he denies the supernatural as a distinct realm which imposes itself as a superaddition to the natural, while at the same time avoiding a pure naturalism divested from within of a dimension of the holy. He does this through his position on the participation of all that is finite in God or the holy, so that the holy or God can appear through creation but never be identified with it. Thus man is grounded in the divine, and the deepest movement of his spirit is towards the recovery of his essential participation in the Godhead.

Jung, too, makes it difficult to conceive of a division between the natural and the supernatural. Rather he shows how the experience of the numinous is made possible through the activation of archetypes in the unconscious. For Jung, the unconscious is the place from which comes man's sense of the divine, and also the source of the movement of man's life towards the self, as consciousness unites with the depths to create a more whole personality. Thus Tillich and Jung locate the reality of the divine within both nature and man, and understand the development of man as a process of growing into this awareness.

Because both men felt that the sense of the intimacy and inevitability of God's presence to man had been lost, with great cost to individual and society, their views warrant a more systematic analysis and correlation. The major points in such a comparison are the positions they take on the nature of religious consciousness and its symbolic expression, God, Christ, the Church, and the future or eschatology. These questions can now be addressed.

2 The Psyche as Sacrament

A sacrament can be described as that reality through which the holy makes its presence felt. From their conviction that man is naturally endowed with a sense of the sacred, it follows that Tillich and Jung understand man's interiority, the depths of reason and the psyche, as that through which the ultimate makes its impact on man; in other words, man experiences the numinous as rising from his own depths. Moreover, both contend that this experience is so great that it defies rational and precise expression and demands the symbol as the only mode of expression adequate to its wealth.[1]

Tillich and Jung are concerned not only about modern man's loss of religious sensitivity, but also about the accompanying loss of a symbolic sense. Both losses are but two aspects of the same impoverishment. As man loses conscious touch with the sacred, he inevitably loses the capacity to appreciate and to respond to the way it is expressed through the symbol. Religiously and theologically, the loss of the symbolic leads to the pathology of literalism. When the mythic is read literally, its true power and meaning are lost. The consequence is that myth itself is eventually dismissed and thereby man loses access to the depths from which it arises. Thus both Tillich and Jung inveigh against a revelation which is "dropped from heaven."[2] Both oppose the trend, especially in Protestant theologies of the Word, to a literalism divested of a sense of the symbolic and mysterious. Tillich continually deplores the fact that it is so common to hear truths which can only be expressed symbolically dismissed with the question " . . . only a symbol?"[3] Jung too wonders what the real gain of demythologizing might be, since myth is the native language or mother tongue of the revelatory experience.[4] The intensity of Jung's concern in this area is reflected in his declared willingness to "fight for symbolic thinking."[5]

The five characteristics Tillich repeatedly attributes to symbols will serve as a point of departure and as a basis of comparison between Tillich and Jung. These characteristics presuppose an elaborate understanding of how intimately man's reason is linked to its depths in God, and so they point to Tillich's whole religious epistemology and to his theology of revelation. The latter is grounded on the interplay of mind at one with its depths, in a state Tillich calls "ecstatic," with an objective counterpart through which the depths of reality appear, which Tillich calls "miracle." The characteristics Tillich attributes to symbols are:[6]

31

1. Both signs and symbols point beyond themselves but signs and symbols are not the same.
2. They differ because symbols participate in that to which they point.
3. Symbols open up levels of reality otherwise closed to consciousness.
4. Symbols open up dimensions of ourselves otherwise closed to us.
5. "Symbols cannot be produced intentionally.... They grow out of the individual or collective unconscious and cannot function without being accepted by the unconscious dimension of our being."[7]

A sixth characteristic Tillich occasionally mentions is that symbols grow and die.[8]

Jung could and does give some kind of agreement to each of these characteristics. Indeed, in places in his work, there are almost verbal coincidences in the way Jung's writing on symbol parallels Tillich's. More than once Jung takes exception to Freud's use of the term symbol to designate a psychosomatic condition, or bodily expression of an inner state. "What Freud terms symbols," he writes, are no more than *signs* for elementary instinctive processes."[9] Jung's point is that Freud's use misses the sense of mystery or surplus of meaning which attaches to a symbol and which differentiates it from a sign. Hence, like Tillich, Jung is of the opinion that a symbol contains an element that defies rational precision.

Tillich distinguishes sign from symbol in his claim that the latter "participates" in that to which it points. Participation as Tillich understands it is indeed a difficult idea to grasp, though it runs as an undercurrent throughout his system. In a most general sense, Tillich means that a symbol is drawn from some segment of finite reality through which the divine has appeared. By this he supposes that all of reality, as grounded in the divine, can be a vehicle for the appearance of the divine. A mind receptive to such transparency is in the state Tillich calls ecstatic. In this sense the symbol is invested with a numinosity grounded in the depths of both mind and outer reality.

For Jung, too, the symbols have a numinous power, though Jung traces this numinosity more to the subjective disposition of the psyche than to an external reality. The symbol for Jung is a bearer or embodiment of the power of the archetypes of the collective unconscious, and points to the energies of the unconscious in their living and changing configurations. These energies and the archetypes from which they flow are experienced not only as numinous but often as suprapersonal, or at least as existing autonomously in relation to ego consciousness. They make their presence known and their power felt through dreams or other imaginal processes. The impact of the symbol on consciousness is so great, according to Jung, that "it seizes and possesses the whole personality, and is naturally productive of faith."[10] The ego can be convinced that the numinosity attaching to the symbol places the ego before the reality of God: "The symbol needs man for its development. But it grows beyond him, therefore it is called 'God' since it expresses a psychic situation or factor stronger than the ego."[11]

Jung also agrees with Tillich that the symbol opens up depths of oneself and one's surroundings previously closed. The symbol, as it appears in dreams or in other products of the unconscious, makes conscious what was previously unconscious and is directly tailored to the need of the individual's process of becoming aware. This heightening of consciousness through contact with its inner source will eventually bring with it a deeper appreciation of and a freer response to one's surrounding reality at all levels.

Tillich and Jung share further similar views on the question of the impossibility of the conscious construction of the symbol. For Jung the symbol is the product of the activation of an archetype in the unconscious. Because he attributes such a high degree of autonomy to the unconscious (relative to the ego), he denies the possibility of the ego deliberately manipulating the unconscious in such a way as to control its products. The unconscious, in Jung's view, works continuously to compensate conscious imbalances and inadequacies, and so will produce symbols addressed to consciousness from a position beyond it and somewhat superior to it. For these reasons Jung writes that a symbol "has a life of its own . . . it cannot be invented or fabricated."[12] For Tillich too the symbol rises to consciousness from an area over which mind and will have no direct manipulative power.

The final characteristic Tillich attributes to symbols is their capacity to grow and to die. When he expands on this point he argues that one faith can only be replaced by another. Since faith, in its initial experiential reality, expresses itself in symbols, one symbol can only be replaced by another. Since symbols cannot be consciously produced, they cannot be consciously replaced in such a way as to capture the depths or faith of those responding to them. A further consequence is that rational criticism, theological or philosophical, cannot kill a symbol which has caught the collective imagination. Only another symbol which grasps the collective mind can do so.

What Tillich is suggesting here is that man is by his nature subjected to the impress of the revelatory and the flow of symbols which arise spontaneously from the depths of his being. Thus human history could be viewed as the history of revelations, each producing its own symbols with their attendant faiths. This points to the inevit-

ability of the revelatory and its accompanying symbols in human
consciousness, and is substantially identical with Jung's claim that
when symbols and their faiths cease to appear in religious guise they
reappear in the "isms" which are the operative faiths in a postreli-
gious age.[13]

In general, then, both men take seriously the symbol- and faith-
engendering forces within life. Yet there are nuances in their appreciation of the symbolic. Both are aware of the collective role of
symbols, functioning religiously or through political ideologies. But
Jung has a more personalized conception, believing that the symbolic world addresses man every night in his sleeping hours. This
dimension is muted in Tillich's thought, concerned mainly with the
collective Christian symbols; as a Christian he holds these to be
somehow definitive and the substance of the "final" revelation.[14] In
all fairness to Tillich it must be added that he believes one only truly
comes into the reality of the symbol of Christ when it grasps and
transforms one with its power (see Chapter 4).

Finally Jung, too, speaks of the birth and death of symbols in a
manner comparable to Tillich. He understands the role or function
of the prophet to be that of bringing to birth, through the depths of
his own person, the symbolic expression or myth that responds to
the spiritual needs and aspirations of the age.[15] Because the myth
addresses the spiritual needs of the time, or even aion, it receives
collective acceptance. But Jung, as does Tillich in certain of his
formulations, points to the relativity of the symbol and to the fact
that a change in the conscious and collective situation can elicit or
occasion a change in the symbol system:

> So long as the symbol is the true and redeeming answer to the
> corresponding situation, it is true and valid, indeed "absolute." But if
> the situation changes and the symbol is simply perpetuated, it is
> nothing but an idol, having an impoverishing and stultifying effect,
> because it merely makes us unconscious and provides no explanation
> and enlightenment.[16]

Tillich makes a very similar point when he writes that "a religious
symbol can die only if the correlation of which it is an adequate
expression dies."[17] That is, it dies only when it ceases to mediate the
ultimate for its holder, understood as either individual or collective.
Tillich continues:

> This occurs whenever the revelatory situation changes and former
> symbols become obsolete. The history of religion, right up to our own
> time, is full of dead symbols which have been killed not by a scientific
> criticism of assumed superstitions but by a religious criticism of reli-
> gions.[18]

The key phrase in that passage is "a religious criticism of religions." In saying this Tillich affirms that only the revelatory or the symbolic is capable of transplanting accepted revelation and its symbols. His thought here again points to the inevitability of the revelatory and the symbolic in human consciousness, but his commitment to the Christian symbols as definitive or final presents a problem to him because nothing but his faithful commitment to these symbols demands that they be final. Though Tillich's theology is based on a universal conception of man as religious and as symbol maker, his commitment to the Christian symbols is due to his faith that in Christ man's essential humanity has appeared and grasped him. Tillich is aware of this option and describes it in terms of the "theological circle."[19] By this he means that the Christian theologian theologizes in the context of Christ as his ultimate concern or object of his faith, and that this involves the Christian theologian in a certain circularity.

On this point the relativity which results from Jung's view of symbols is less embarrassed by the multiplicity of dead symbols and religions, and less constrained to attribute finality to the Christian symbol system. It is freer to trace similarities between some of the main features of the Christian religion and other religions or "families" of gods.

*

An examination of the epistemology underlying Tillich's thought on symbol reveals an intimacy of the mind to God. This parallels Jung's thought on the relationship of the ego to its depths in the unconscious, from which it derives its sense of the numinous.

Tillich distinguishes three levels of reason. If one were to grade them from the more superficial to the deeper and more significant, they would run from technical or controlling reason, to ontological reason, to the depth of reason. Technical or controlling reason refers to the capacity of the mind to order means to ends, and so to control or manipulate external reality in man's interests. The exercise of this faculty implies a cognitive distance from the known and controlled; this distance divests the object of its subjectivity, and of any Eros which might be conferred upon it by its knower. Tillich expresses strong reservations about the modern fascination with technical reason (including logical positivism) and technology, for they remove man from the deeper structures of his mind and so from those symbols through which ultimate meaning can enter his life. Technical reason "dehumanizes man" when it pervades the world of the humanities and of philosophy wherein the meaning of man and his world is directly addressed.[20]

Because it divests a person of his subjectivity, technical reason tends to cause rather than alleviate pathology. The extent of Tillich's antipathy towards this use of the mind is revealed when he writes:

> A consequence of this attitude is a rapid decay of spiritual life.... In psychology and sociology, in medicine and philosophy, man has been dissolved into elements out of which he is composed and which determine him.... Man actually has become what controlling knowledge considers him to be, a thing among things, a cog in the dominating machine of production and consumption, a dehumanized object of tyranny or a normalized object of public communications. Cognitive dehumanization has produced actual dehumanization.[21]

This declamation of Tillich's strikes a certain resonance with those passages in which Jung denounces a "psychology without the psyche,"[22] and insists that psychology, even as a science, must relate to the subjectivity of the individual in order to address the soul. An important implication of this view is that only that which is loved can be known.

Passing to the next level, Tillich understands ontological reason to be the structure of mind and of reality which allows the former to grasp and shape the latter and the latter to be grasped and shaped by the former. As do most epistemologists, Tillich distinguishes between subjective and objective structures of ontological reason, and locates the origin of knowledge in their interaction, that is, in the interaction of the structure of the mind with the structure of reality. Again, like most classical epistemologists, Tillich understands knowledge as working towards a union between knower and known which yet preserves their distance or distinction. Here again Tillich introduces the idea that only that which is known through love is truly known. He argues that if one knows only in terms of distancing the object from oneself, then that knowledge can reduce the thing or person known to the status of an object as does controlling knowledge. And for Tillich, "No thing, however, is merely a thing."[23] This means that the thing known must also be received by, or made the object of, a gnosis in which it is not only known but loved in such a way that the knower is gripped by it and responds to it holistically, a response that combines knowledge and love.

At this point Tillich approaches the problem of reason in its essential and existential aspects. His contention here is somewhat radical. He identifies reason in its essential reality with the content of revelation. By this he means that the ontological structure of the mind in its essential reality is at one with the divine as grounded in the Logos, the principle of God's self-definition and the possibility of God's expression beyond himself:

> Since God is the ground of being, he is the ground of the structure of being. He is not subject to the structure; the structure is grounded in him. He *is* this structure, and it is impossible to speak about him except in terms of this structure.[24]

Thus Tillich takes the position that the essential mind is at one with that side of the ground of being that is the principle of structure both within and beyond God. In other words, everything that participates in structure participates in the Logos character of God.

However, like all of reality, reason too, in its existential or actual state, is fallen; that is, it lives and functions away from its essential source and basis in God, though never so far away that it ever loses real and experienceable continuity with it. Reason's groundedness in God is what Tillich means by the term "depth of reason," which precedes reason in its more normal or common functions and appears in man's sense of the absolute. Man's depth of reason gives rise to a sense of absolute truth in relation to pure cognition, absolute beauty in relation to aesthetic reason, absolute justice in relation to legal reason, and absolute love in the realm of communal reason.[25]

When such absolute power surges through the structure of reason in existence, it can only be expressed in symbol and myth and acted out in cult. To make this point Tillich sometimes uses strange and striking formulations. Reason in existence is at once so near and so far from its essential unity with God, that when it experiences this unity latent in itself it must use symbolic and mythical formulations to express it. The necessity to express this experience symbolically betrays reason's unity with and distance from God—unity because such experience is possible, and distance because the experience of this unity cannot be expressed with clarity and precision. Tillich succinctly captures this predicament:

> Because of these conditions reason in existence expresses itself in myth and cult as well as in its proper functions. There should be neither myth nor cult. They contradict essential reason; they betray by their very existence the "fallen" state of reason which has lost immediate unity with its own depth.[26]

With this model of reason as latently at one with God in its depths, Tillich is then in a position to describe the processes in which revelation can and indeed must occur. Ontological reason, both as the subjective structure of the mind and as objective structure of the extramental, is susceptible to being invaded by its own depths. Such invasion is for Tillich the actualization of a natural latency of reason which constitutes revelation.

In describing the revelatory event, Tillich uses three categories based on the different levels of reason. The categories are mystery, ecstasy, and miracle. "The genuine mystery appears when reason is driven beyond itself."[27] Tillich describes this condition in various ways, but basically in terms of reason's entry into the abyss dimension within the Godhead as somehow preceding all structures and support. The circumstance of the mind being driven beyond itself is its experience of "the stigma of finitude"[28] and "the threat of nonbeing."[29] This is the initiatory experience that drives reason beyond its usual operations, and only as a consequence of this threat to the existence of reason and its holder does the ground of being appear as supportive.

This crisis that serves as the occasion for the appearance of mystery has some affinity with Jung's understanding that symbols arise from the depths of the psyche when the ego is under some type of pressure or tension—as when caught between logically irreconcilable opposites which have crippled or to some extent paralysed the ego. Such a psychic crisis serves as the precondition for the reconciling and life-restoring symbol (in Jung's terms, the transcendent function) which moves consciousness to a broader, more comprehensive perspective. Thus Jung and Tillich both point to the genesis of the symbol as frequently, if not necessarily, preceded and accompanied by "the shaking of the foundations" of normal consciousness.

Tillich expands on his conception of the dynamics of the revelatory by showing how both subjective and objective reason correlate in such a situation. He argues that revelation occurs when the depth of reason appears through subjective reason throwing the mind into a state of ecstasy. In this subjective state the perception of reality as miracle occurs: "The mystery appears objectively in terms of what traditionally has been called 'miracle.' It appears subjectively in terms of what has sometimes been called 'ecstasy.'"[30]

Tillich describes ecstasy as a state of mind in which reason is beyond itself but does not destroy itself. Thus he speaks of a destructive or demonic ecstasy in which the mind loses itself in forms of inebriation or in states of religious solipsism or overexcitement. Sometimes he describes it in terms of a part of the mind seizing the whole and so destroying its balance, which is close to Jung's view of evil psychologically as a state of "possession" of the ego by an autonomous complex or archetype.

Tillich feels that since such ecstasy involves a loss of mind it is inevitably dehumanizing. However, because he conceives of the essential structures of reason as grounded in God, Tillich can conceive of a situation in which subjective reason can go beyond the normal subject-object split in which it usually functions and attain a unity with that which precedes the split, namely the reality of the divine in which both subject and object inhere. Consequently ecstatic reason, in its intersection with its divine depths, can perceive, in however attenuated a manner, the divine depths in reality beyond itself. Out of this situation of depth calling to depth, revelation and its symbols arise.

Tillich can give a certain overriding description of the content of such an experience. From the viewpoint of subjective reason, the mystery follows upon an "ontological shock," provoked by reason's experience of the negativities which attach to its finitude and to its existential plight.[31] This experience of shock or stigma is the initiation into the revelation of the mystery. At times Tillich writes as if part of this shock is the realization, on the part of reason itself, of the tremendous or overwhelming aspect of the Deity, in the face of which one's finitude is consumed. This moment in the experience of the *mysterium tremendum* within the Godhead is complemented by the experience of the *mysterium fascinosum,* the meaningful, expressive, and supportive side of the divine life.[32]

But the experience of inherence in the divine ground remains both ambivalent and lively. The God who appears to reason out of its depths as its ground is thus a God made up of powerful opposites which both overwhelm and support the mind that comes into contact with them.

It is difficult to escape the conclusion here that man's natural experience of God is of a life force made up of opposite poles and so is naturally Trinitarian. Nor is this God so distant from the one depicted by Jung in his *Answer to Job,* where God both overwhelms and supports Job and seems ultimately to move towards the balance and integration of spirit. In short, both Tillich and Jung locate in man's experience of God the basis for Trinitarian symbolism.

Where Tillich and Jung differ somewhat in their views on the generation of symbol is over the question of the objective aspect of the experience. Jung, in certain of his formulations, implies that man can experience revelation simply by directing his energies inwards, as in what he calls active imagination. However, elsewhere Jung describes revelatory situations in terms of the correlation between an expectation developing in the unconscious and a man, prophet or messiah, who can serve as the object of this expectation. Here Jung is closer to the way in which Tillich correlates the mind in ecstasy and the objective miracle which is always in constellation with it. Tillich at times calls the objective side of the revelatory constellation a sign event. By this term he means that the divine can appear through the objective structures of reality, just as it can appear in the subjective structures of mind, without destroying them because the objective structure of extramental reality is also grounded in the divine.

Thus for Tillich a miracle is not a demonic interference in the structures of creation by a God who must destroy the structures he creates in order to appear in them as revealer. Rather the miracle of revelation occurs when the structures of objective reality become transparent to their depths, just as ecstasy occurs when the mind becomes transparent to its divine depths. For Tillich both aspects of the mystery must appear in correlation. Mind in ecstasy perceives reality as miracle.

Based on these epistemological principles, Tillich sets forth certain norms which determine the validity of a revelatory event. Such events must be gripping without destroying reason; otherwise they would lack revelatory power. They must point to the truly ultimate; otherwise they could be the result of sorcery or the mere manipulation of reason. They must be received by a mind in ecstasy; otherwise the mind is not experientially engaged in the events but is responding to a revelation and its symbols that have occurred in the experience of another.

Thus the basic Tillichian position reduces to the proposition that "ecstasy is the miracle of the mind and miracle is the ecstasy of reality."[33]

As a Christian theologian, Tillich takes as the prime example of his principles the revelation which occurred when the meaning of Christ was realized by Peter. Jesus asked Peter who he was. Peter answered, "The Christ." Jesus replied that Peter's capacity to discern this truth was because Peter himself was in the Spirit. In Tillich's terms this means that Peter was in a state of ecstasy wherein his mind, at one with its depths, was able to perceive in Jesus the latter's unbroken continuity with his Father, the source of all being.[34]

*

Like Tillich, Jung was dismayed by modern man's loss of a sense for the symbolic, particularly among religious spokesmen and theologians. One can detect a harsh note when he writes:

> It is as necessary today as it ever was to lead the libido away from the cult of rationalism and realism—not, indeed, because these things have gained the upper hand (quite the contrary), but because the guardians and custodians of symbolical truth, namely the religions, have been robbed of their efficacy by science. Even intelligent people no longer understand the value and purpose of symbolical truth, and

the spokesmen of religion have failed to deliver an apologetic suited to the spirit of the age.[35]

Faced with this situation Jung called for a revivification of the sense of the symbolic by the theological community itself, in the interests of a deeper appreciation of its own revelation. In Jung's opinion this would involve rational reflection, such as carried out by Tillich, on precisely why humanity needs the unlikely kind of statement about reality that the symbolic and the mythical express:

> That means placing symbolical truth on a new foundation—a foundation which appeals not only to sentiment, but to reason. And this can only be achieved by reflecting how it came about in the first place that humanity needed the improbability of religious statements, and what it signifies when a totally different spiritual reality is superimposed on the sensuous and tangible actuality of this world.[36]

In these lines Jung shows the same awareness that prompts Tillich to write that "there should be neither myth nor cult," because they involve mental functions that defy the precision and clarity the rational mind is so fond of.[37] And so like Tillich Jung thinks it of great importance to understand why man is driven to be a maker of symbol and myth, and how these realities function in his psychic life.

As early as 1912, Jung expressed the belief that symbol formation was grounded in the archetypes of the collective unconscious. From these "primordial images," unknowable in themselves, symbols rise to consciousness with the same numinosity that invariably accompanies religious experience. These symbols make a powerful impact on consciousness precisely because they come from so deep a layer of the psyche. Speaking of the power of Christ's teaching Jung writes: "The reason why Jesus' words have such great suggestive power is that they express the symbolical truths which are rooted in the very structure of the human psyche."[38] As a therapist Jung thus felt it necessary to point his patients to the inner sources of healing in the psyche which constitute at the same time the basis of religious experience. He writes, "The medical psychotherapist today must make clear to his more educated patients the foundations of religious experience, and set them on the road to where such an experience becomes possible."[39]

Jung confesses an interest in religious symbols strictly for therapeutic purposes. His aim, he writes, is "to enable people to think symbolically once more."[40] For Jung the recovery of such a capacity is the precondition for again participating "spiritually in the substance of the Christian message."[41] The point Jung makes is that Christians, in understanding their myth and its symbols literally, have lost both the spiritual impact of these symbols and contact with their own deeper humanity from which the symbols arise and to which they should lead. A further consequence of what Jung says here is that the specifically Christian symbols are universal, at least potentially, and hence should appear both prior to and beyond their specifically Christian expression.

In certain passages in his early works Jung expresses concern that the Christian symbols will be discarded by society with nothing to replace them, and so with nothing to prevent the brutality that follows upon a life without the containment and channeling of libido (psychic energy) offered by the symbols.[42] But if either the Christian or any other symbol system is to offer man a humane containment for his energies, which can so easily become barbaric, then a new appreciation and a heightened experience of the symbolic world becomes necessary. Man would once again have to find a faith that is more than an intellectual assent to the "sacrosanct unintelligibility" of an authoritarian doctrine.[43] Man would have to find the lifegiving and containing symbol, whether Christian or not, in his own experience. "'Legitimate' faith," writes Jung, "must always rest on experience."[44] In this Jung aligns himself with Tillich's understanding of faith as ultimate concern; for both it is based on an experiential factor.

For Jung the symbols arising from the unconscious have not only a religious meaning or power but also act as curative and wholemaking:

> Since faith revolves around those central and perennially important 'dominant ideas' which alone give life a meaning, the prime task of the psychotherapist must be to understand the symbols anew, and thus to understand the unconscious, compensatory striving of his patient for an attitude that reflects the totality of the psyche.[45]

Thus Jung clearly locates the genesis of faith in the archetypes that reveal themselves through "dominant ideas," which later he calls symbols and which work to heal by giving to consciousness the balance it needs to become whole. Indeed, so convinced is Jung of the internal origins of religious reality that he writes that if the religions were eliminated today, they would be reborn from within tomorrow: "One could almost say that if all the world's traditions were cut off at a single blow, the whole of mythology and the whole history of religion would start all over again with the next generation."[46]

Like Tillich, Jung goes to some lengths to be precise about the origin of symbols. He frequently speaks of them as rising "up from the creative unconscious of the living man."[47] He understands religious devotion as "a regressive movement of libido towards the primordial, a diving down into the source of the first beginnings."[48] So Jung's thought on symbol has a very profound side, linked to the mystical experience of the inner God. Since it is through the symbol that the archetypal becomes conscious, it is also through the symbol that man becomes conscious of God—and, adds Jung, that God, through human consciousness, becomes conscious of Himself.

Here he enters into the mystical domain and quotes Meister Eckhart with obvious approval. Jung understands that symbols derive from the activation of the archetypes and that this can be aided by man's deliberate direction of his energies inwards upon them. Speaking of Eckhart's experience, Jung states that "the soul is a personification of the unconscious, where lies the treasure, the libido which is immersed in introversion and is allegorized as God's kingdom."[49] Thus the ability to direct one's energies inwards can be the occasion of the activation of man's experience of himself as image of God.[50] This makes man conscious of God and God real in man's consciousness on a potentially enduring basis. Describing the mystical experience Jung writes: "This amounts to a permanent union with God, a living in his kingdom, in that state where a preponderance of libido lies in the unconscious and determines conscious life."[51] This state is described by Jung as the experience of God no longer working from without but from within.[52]

In speaking of the soul (or anima) and its role in symbol formation, Jung places it in a mediational role between consciousness and the unconscious, so that it belongs partly to each realm, or as Jung puts it, "partly to the subject and partly to the world of spirits, i.e., the unconscious."[53] In this schema the soul is not a substance or a static identity. Rather it is "a function of relation between the subject and the inaccessible depths of the unconscious."[54] Here also Jung is most explicit that the symbols which provide man with the experience of God proceed from the unconscious through the soul into consciousness:

> The determining force (God) operating from these depths is reflected by the soul, that is, it creates symbols and images, and is itself only an image. By means of these images the soul conveys the forces of the unconscious to consciousness; it is both receiver and transmitter, an organ for perceiving unconscious contents. What it perceives are symbols.[55]

In these words Jung implies that the soul is a subsistent relation, the quality of which is determined by the quality of its symbols and its relation to the poles it mediates—consciousness on the one hand and the unconscious on the other. Jung cites Eckhart to the effect that when the soul is in God it is not blissful, which Jung interprets to mean a state of soul that has lost its relation to consciousness. On the other hand, when God is in the soul then Jung understands that "the soul becomes a vessel for the unconscious and makes itself an image or symbol of it...a truly happy state."[56] Elsewhere Jung describes this state as one in which "the regenerated attitude, the libido, that was formerly sunk in the unconscious emerges in the form of some positive achievement."[57]

Jung, in these passages, is not only defining the soul as a living relation that mediates symbols from the unconscious to consciousness, he is also contending that man's experience of God and God's becoming conscious of Himself in human consciousness are made possible through the mediation of the soul. In this model of the psyche, man relates to God as does the ego to the unconscious. Thus Jung identifies Eckhart's use of the term "Godhead" with the blind power of the unconscious, and suggests that from this more remote source, through the mediation of the soul, the symbol of God proceeds into consciousness. Hence, in Jung's view, the soul naturally "declares" the reality of God since the symbol of itself as image of God is native to it.[58]

This aspect of Jung's thought is another instance of his general alignment with the ontological argument, which in the history of Western civilization has consistently sought to invest man with an immediate sense of the reality of God in some aspect of human interiority.

The process of symbol formation Jung describes in the context of Eckhart's mysticism is closely related to his understanding of the flow of psychic energy. As the libido is directed inwards in a regressive movement, it divests the ego of its energy and so induces states of depression. The ego sinks into the unconscious where it meets the *deus absconditus,* the dark and chthonic powers of the unconscious.[59] But from these depths it is reborn in the flow of psychic energy Jung calls progression. With this rebirth ego consciousness has a heightened sense of its unity with a supporting and energizing source, which can be experienced as the reality of the divine. This is the process of God being born in the soul of man.[60] It is also the basis of Jung's attraction to the poetry of Angelus Silesius, which illustrates the intimate connection between man's ego and his divine depths, a relation of complementarity if not completion:

I know that without me
God can no moment live;
Were I to die, then He
No longer could survive.

I am as great as God,
And He is small like me;
He cannot be above,
Nor I below Him be.[61]

The symbol in its function of uniting the unconscious and conscious levels of the psyche—in the interest of bringing about a balanced and broadened consciousness and a renewed flow of psychic
energies—is part and parcel of what Jung calls the transcendent
function. Jung closely relates psychic energies to the conflicts which
often occur between the attitude of the ego and that of the unconscious. The opposites can be so sharply constellated that the psyche
is driven to search for "a third" which can reconcile or unify the
apparently irremediable conflict. In this state of psychic tension the
numinous symbol can provide consciousness with a new attitude or
perspective which transcends and resolves the warring opposites.[62]
Such a symbolic manifestation is always very personal and always
has a powerful impact. In this it would be comparable to certain
aspects Tillich attributes to the symbol and to its relation to faith, in
that the meaning of the symbol is experientially assimilated.

Where Jung differs from Tillich is in his emphasis on the highly
personal significance of the symbol. He agrees with Tillich that
symbols cannot be consciously constructed, they are "always produced out of the unconscious by way of revelation or intuition."[63]
But Jung is more concerned with the revelatory symbols that emerge
from the individual's contact with his own unconscious, aimed at the
solution of a particular life problem. Thus he deplores the fact that
the formation of state religions and the abolition of polytheism has
brought about "the suppression of individual symbol-formation."[64]

This has many implications. For instance, when the collective
symbol system fails an individual, it may be necessary for him or her
to rely for a time or permanently on the more immediate contact
available with the sacred through the symbols which come to consciousness from his or her personal contact with the unconscious. In
addition, contact with the unconscious could serve as a critical tool
in the evaluation of the prevailing myth or symbol system. (This is
happening currently in the controversy over the role of the feminine
in the Christian myth.) On the other hand, experience of one's own
symbols could deepen the appreciation of the collective symbol
which one has previously accepted. Or, finally, it could enhance
one's appreciation of the symbolic import of the religious and religions as such.

However, it is clear that Jung equates "the making of a religion"
with "the formation of symbols."[65] He states that when a reductive

psychoanalysis has reached the limit of its possibilities, a synthetic process follows in which the symbol can function as a new religious perspective, or as Jung terms it, "a religion of individual character."[66] This is not actually an attack on collective religion. Jung clearly states that "for a long time and for the great majority of mankind the symbol of a collective religion will suffice."[67] He also suggests that in many cases contact with one's personal symbol and myth may only be temporarily necessary, to allow one to become conscious of one's distinctiveness.[68]

Referring to the transcendent function, Jung writes: "It is called 'transcendent' because it makes the transition from one attitude to another organically possible without loss of the unconscious."[69] This new attitude, which is brought about in large part through holding the tension between the opposites, Jung describes as "a living birth that leads to a new level of being, a new situation."[70] Jung further speaks of this new attitude in terms that echo Tillich. According to Jung such a transformed perspective enables one to find "the courage to be oneself."[71] Similarly, in *The Courage To Be,* Tillich presents a picture of man seeking the courage to be, in the face of the tensions involved in death, guilt, and meaninglessness.[72] Ultimately Tillich locates the source of the courage to be in man's experience of the support of God as the ground or power of his being. But he often implies that man comes to experience these depths as supportive only to the extent that he first fully experiences the negations or difficulties in life.

Jung and Tillich also agree that the symbols mediating to man his hoped-for courage to be are never of an unqualified clarity, though they are filled with a redemptive power. In a passage on the mysterious yet envigorating nature of the symbol, Jung strikes a note that would find many a resonance in Tillich. "A symbol really lives," he writes, "only when it is the best and highest expression for something divined but not yet known to the observer. It then compels his unconscious participation and has a life-giving and life-enhancing effect."[73] Moreover, it proceeds from and unites the many opposites in man and in particular the opposites of matter and spirit. In other words, it must combine "man's highest spiritual aspirations" while "at the same time spring from the deepest roots of his being."[74]

Thus Tillich and Jung held the symbolic life in the highest esteem. For both the symbol provided man with access to a higher and balanced humanity, experienced as much as gift as accomplishment. They agree that the symbol comes into consciousness when the personality is under strain, and that its effect is to heal suffering. With Tillich this occurs when the mind is confronted with its own relative nothingness, the precondition for the experience of the sustaining force of the Godhead. With Jung the symbol arises to meet an imbalance or a split in the personality. For both the symbol rises to meet man in such a way as to give him an experience of the unity that lies beyond the opposites.

These similarities must be contrasted with differences in emphasis. Tillich is more concerned with the collective Christian symbol of Christ, and less conscious of the reality of one's personal symbols and the way they may complement the collective symbol system. But even on this point Tillich's theology works to show how the reality of Christ meets the inner demand of man for his essential humanity. Tillich's depth of reason corresponds in a significant way with Jung's conception of the collective unconscious, since both terms refer to the ultimate source of man's residual sense of God.

In any event both thinkers picture the human ego as fragile and as extended over an infinite abyss which can shake and transform it, and hopefully show to it an ultimately benign and healing face. This life in the depths, this power which seems to force itself upon consciousness in times of crisis, may be called the collective unconscious or the ground and power of being, but the reality thus designated functions with the force of the divine.

3 God, the Union of Opposites, and the Trinity

If Tillich and Jung are concerned to show how the religious symbol arises from man's depths under certain conditions of tension, it is because both locate the reality of God within man. From this position they affirm that man's sense of divine transcendence derives from certain aspects of his self-consciousness. Jung and Tillich believe that what the Christian symbols make explicit are experiences of the ultimate. With Tillich, this is based on man's native participation in God; with Jung, on man's experience of the power of the archetypal symbols arising from the unconscious.

How radically both men take the inner wellsprings of man's sense of God is revealed in the way they discuss the symbol of the Trinity. This is usually held by more conservative theologies to be the primary example of revelation totally from beyond, lacking any basis in human experience. But for Tillich and Jung the dynamic symbolized by the Trinity arises from man's depth experience of his own life processes, human and divine.

For Tillich life is made up of the flow of energy between opposing poles or opposites. These opposites are in constant threat of tragic disruption, with the consequent possibility that life will disintegrate. But Tillich believes the opposites of human life are grounded in divine life, where their tension is present but present as overcome.[1] This divine life constantly proffers to human life the unity of its opposites, first made real through the Spirit. For Jung the symbol of the Trinity rises from the flow of energy between man's ego and its unconscious matrix. As the psyche enters into this flow it participates in an energy and balance of opposites which is experienced as of the divine; a symbol such as the mandala is a universal expression of this experience of balanced centredness (either actual or longed for).

Tillich, speaking as a theologian, takes the stance that historically the symbol of the Trinity arose from the event of Christ and the Christian reflection upon it.[2] This reflection came to relate Christ to the Father as somehow preceding and sending him, and to the Spirit as following and sent by him. But Tillich goes on to ground the Christian formulation of the Trinity on two factors that attach to man's universal religious experience, and provide the natural basis in life for the reception of the revelation. The first factor is the tension between man's experience of God as absolute and as concrete; the second, of more interest in relation to Jung, is man's intuitive experience of the opposites in the divine life which grounds his own. These two factors lead to a necessary formulation of God as Trinitarian. Tillich writes, "In this sense we can say that the trinitarian symbols are a religious discovery which had to be made, formulated, and defended."[3]

For Tillich neither the concrete nor the transcendent is in itself adequate to the needs of the human spirit. Man's earliest religious experience placed the ultimate in the concrete and so in a multiplicity of things. Man had many gods. Polytheism reigned but tore man apart by subjecting him to many, conflicting ultimates or gods. The resulting tension led to the positing of a God beyond all concretion in a unified, transcendent absolute. Thus the counter-tendency to polytheism gave rise to monotheism, which placed the reality of the divine so far beyond man that it was divested of sensible reality and so of the possibility of personal manifestation to man. But man's very need for some manifestation of the ultimate gave birth to mediators capable of appearing visibly and often in human form. These mediators run the gamut, in Tillich's view, from personalized divine attributes, such as Wisdom or Sophia, through the angelic to such divine-human figures as Christ. Yet all serve the same purpose. They concretize the transcendent God and result in a triadic conception of Him, the poles or principles of which would be divine transcendence, its concrete and personal manifestation, and the bond of unity or relatedness between them. Tillich describes this dynamic as follows:

> The concreteness of man's ultimate concern drives him toward polytheistic structures; the reaction of the absolute element against these drives him toward monotheistic structures; and the need for a balance between the concrete and the absolute drives him toward trinitarian structures.[4]

For the Christian this process culminates with Christ as the final mediator, who in the confines of an historical personal life relates in unbroken unity to the Father in the Spirit and so, in Tillich's categories, realizes essential humanity in the conditions of existence.[5]

Tillich's description of the second basis of man's Trinitarian experience within life appears even closer to certain aspects of Jung's thought. Both conceive of God as a *coincidentia oppositorum*. With Tillich this conception is based on life itself as made up of the coincidence of opposites, which in turn are grounded in God as both the source of the opposites which constitute human life and the source of their unification in balanced growth.

To elaborate Tillich's position on God's presence to life as source and unifier of opposites requires some examination of his thought on creation and fall, and two concepts he closely relates to creation and fall, namely essence and existence.

Tillich locates essential being in a living and so Trinitarian God. More specifically he locates the essential structures of being in the Logos, as the adequate expression within the Godhead of all that can have definition in creation and so existence beyond the Godhead. Essential being as thus expressed within the Godhead in the process of divine self-definition is eternal, and is the expression of all structure which can exist beyond the Godhead. Yet this expression of divine power in the Logos remains within the Godhead simply potential. Thus essential humanity and the essence of each human remain as expressed in the Logos in a state of unactualized essence, perfect though unrealized in existence, a state Tillich terms "dreaming innocence."[6]

The progression of the essential beyond its pristine expression within the Godhead is the reality of creation. But when the essential steps out of its basis in the Godhead it also falls away from it. In this way fall and creation are inextricably connected, descriptions of two sides of the process of the realization of humanity in existence. To exist away from God is both to exist in a state of creation beyond the Godhead and so be real, and yet to fall from an unqualified unity with God. Thus for Tillich the reality of existence is directly related to man's distance from God, a distance he universally confirms by the use of his will.

But the key point Tillich makes is that man, even in his existential distance from God and in the distortions of his humanity which follow therefrom, never wholly loses his essential connection or rootedness in the divine matrix from which he has proceeded into creation; thus is preserved in existence, however ambiguously, man's essential participation in the being of God.[7]

It is this inherence of the mind in God which makes possible and necessary man's sense of the ultimate in life. In this way Tillich grounds the inevitability of man's concern with the ultimate in man's experience of God as the ground of his being with which he is essentially at one but from which he is existentially alienated. The experience of this ground can be powerful when it manifests, usually in a life crisis, but it remains ambiguous because the mind in existence is never wholly at one with its essential source.

To capture his sense of the intimacy, indeed, interpenetration, of the divine and the human, Tillich often uses the expression "ground of being." This describes God's relation to man in such a way as to imply that God is the cause of man and the substance of man, while denying that God causes man from a distance, as a potter makes a pot. It also denies that the ontological continuity between man and God constitutes a substantial identity.[8] The latter position is one understanding of pantheism which Tillich cannot accept because it allows for no sense of God and man transcending each other. Though God be the ground of creation and of man He can never be reduced to either. A residue of transcendence always remains, and so God remains more than His expression in creation while His expression in creation remains in part beyond Him.

The establishment of such intimate connections between man and God also allows Tillich to contend that man's sense of God bears with it a premonition of God as triadic, in that it constitutes a natural experience of the living God in the depths of his abyss dimension and in the force of his self-definition in Logos.

According to Tillich, the work of unifying the opposites in both divine and human life is the work of the Spirit. Whatever is held together in any life is done so by Spirit. Such life centred by the Spirit is present in its fullness in God, and in fragment in man under the ambiguities of existence. But because human life is essentially grounded in divine life, it always participates to some extent in the balance and centredness of the divine. Hence the depths of human life constantly proffer to it the possibility of the integration of its opposites and so of its fulfillment.

Tillich argues that man intuits the movements of divine life and the divine Spirit as the unifying principle of divine life. The major polarities man discerns in the divine as the "ground of life" are abyss and meaning, united in Spirit.[9] Tillich refers to God as Spirit uniting power and meaning.[10] Thus he understands the divine life as power constantly giving form or meaning to itself, and form constantly renewing itself in its infinite source. Both movements are mediated by Spirit and, in Tillich's sense, *are* Spirit. (This is dealt with more fully in Chapter 5.)

Tillich is quite precise in defining three major pairs of opposites that characterize life, both human and divine. These opposites are all variations of self and other, which Tillich establishes as the underlying polarity. He calls these poles the "ontological elements."[11] The ontological elements are made up of three sets of polarities, namely individualization and participation, dynamics and form, and freedom and destiny. Each of the opposites in these polarities Tillich grounds in the divine life in such a way that in the Godhead they are real but not destructively divisive because unified in Spirit within the Trinitarian flow. In this way he can describe God as absolute individual and yet as universal participant, as unlimited power giving itself perfectly adequate expression (the major motif in his thought on God as Spirit uniting power and form), and as absolute freedom destined to be so.[12] Tillich uses the first side of these polarities, namely individualization, dynamics, and freedom to ground man's sense of God as personal, and the second side—participation, form, and destiny—to ground man's sense of God as suprapersonal.[13]

Man as a creature participates only ambiguously in the divine life and so in the harmony of these structures. In his life in existence these polarities tend to split or to absorb one another, with the consequence that life fragments into deadly one-sidedness. The individual cannot participate and ends in unrelated and self-enclosed solipsism. Or else he loses himself in participation in the world and cannot regain himself. Man can fail to give form to his potentialities and so dissipate his capacities in a formless life. Or, on the other hand, he can strangle himself with a formalism that becomes inadequate to the demands of his growth. He can use his freedom to deny his destiny in various ways. He may give up his freedom to a tyranny that promises him his destiny in return. He can refuse to take seriously his freedom and the need to align it with a deeper purpose or movement in life. On the other hand he may be born into circumstances of destiny that seriously hamper the possibility of ever growing into his freer humanity. And in many cases the improper use of freedom becomes a negative side of one's destiny.

Tillich's theological conception of God as the ground of man's being, and Spirit as the uniting factor, is very similar to Jung's understanding of those forces within the psyche which work to unite opposites, and so to expand and enhance life. These forces involve the self, especially as it functions to reconcile or accommodate the two great opposites, the ego and the unconscious. In Jung's model the opposite is also true: ego and unconscious working together are in fact a manifestation of the self. The dynamic operative is therefore naturally triadic. Thus for Jung the symbol of the Trinity not only arises out of the psyche but seems to be grounded on its most basic flow of energy, that between the ego and the unconscious. He writes that the symbol of the Trinity "stands in a relationship of living reciprocity to the psyche, whence it originated in the first place,"[14] and adds: "Arrangement in triads is an archetype in the history of religion, which in all probability formed the basis of the Christian Trinity."[15] Like Tillich he wonders how so common and natural a symbol could be understood as imposed on life from without: "It is difficult to understand what could have induced Protestant theologians, whenever possible, to make it appear that the world of Christian ideas dropped straight out of heaven."[16]

Rather than fear or deny an archetypal and so psychic basis for such symbols and beliefs, Christian dogma would in Jung's eyes be

"considerably enhanced" if its archetypal basis were to be acknowledged.[17] He points out that the formulations of Christian dogma are
archetypal precisely because they have been "believed always, every-
where, and by everybody"[18] (a reference to the Vincentian canon).
The spirit of these remarks is that the Christian should be reassured,
rather than threatened, to discover that his symbols arise from the
structure of the psyche itself, because "once having sprung forth
from the unconscious of the human race (and not just in Asia
Minor!), they could rearise anywhere at any time."[19]

Jung's work on the Trinity gives a centrality to the spirit and how
it functions that is comparable to Tillich's view. Tillich sees Spirit as
the fullest expression of God, as a statement of the unity of the
opposites of power and meaning in the Godhead. Jung too sees in
the spirit a certain culmination of the Trinitarian process, in that the
spirit unites father and son and partakes of both. But in this analysis
Jung is primarily using psychological categories. The father charac-
terizes for him a world of undifferentiated unity and so of unconsciousness. It corresponds to the state of the personality prior to the
development of the ego. Once the ego is differentiated and "incarnate" over against the father, this pristine unconscious unity is broken and a polarity results, with attendant tension.

From Jung's psychological perspective this describes the emergence of the ego or son from the unconscious-father, and so is also a
description of the tension that ensues in the relation between the ego
and its unconscious matrix, here designated as the world of the
father. The spirit unites these opposites and brings the process of
differentiation to a fitting culmination in a restored unity:

> As [the spirit] is the third term common to Father and Son, he puts an
> end to the duality, the "doubt" in the Son. He is, in fact, the third
> element that rounds out the Three and restores the One. The point is
> that the unfolding of the One reaches its climax in the Holy Ghost
> after polarizing itself as Father and Son.[20]

From this passage it is clear that for Jung one of the major
meanings of spirit (or Spirit) refers to the unity of unconscious and
conscious. This unification is also a description of the process of
individuation and the formation of the self, the *telos* or direction
native to the psyche in its development. In this quite precise sense
the movement of the psyche towards its maturation is towards spirit.

The full import of Jung's thought in this respect can be further
drawn out. He quotes with approval a medieval text which takes an
Augustinian position on the Trinity as reflected in the structure and
working of the mind itself.[21] The mind is thought of as reflecting a
Trinitarian dynamic in its working, in that intellect, the first princi-

ple of the mind, expresses itself in wisdom and is united to its expression in love. In this sense the mind's natural dynamic is triadic. Jung goes beyond this medieval comparison of the working of the mind to that of the Trinity, and shows how the reciprocity between the unconscious and consciousness is also triadic and so an image of the triadic God. He distinguishes the position of the modern from that of the medieval in these words: "The medieval mind finds it natural to derive the structure of the psyche from the Trinity, whereas the modern mind reverses the procedure."[22] This means that the modern derives the structure of the Trinity from some experience of psychic reality.

Jung locates this experience in the realization of the unity of the opposites of the ego and its unconscious matrix; in the process of individuation this is experienced as a participation in the flow and balance of life. This experience is similar if not identical with Tillich's description of man's experience of the unification of the opposites in his life through a deeper participation in the life of God as the ground of his being.

For Jung the process of individuation is itself intrinsically religious in that the assimilation by the ego of its unconscious resources and energies is an "incarnation." He writes that "self-realization—to put it in religious or metaphysical terms—amounts to God's incarnation."[23] Not only is individuation a sacred process, but the suffering attached to it is equivalent in Jung's view to suffering at the hands of God, and so is the functional equivalent of the suffering of atonement:

> As a result of the integration of conscious and unconscious, [man's] ego enters the "divine" realm, where it participates in "God's suffering." The cause of the suffering is in both cases the same, namely "incarnation," which on the human level appears as "individuation."[24]

In dealing with the spirit Jung opens up new possibilities in the theme of God's intimacy with man. The spirit would seem to be a religious personification of the relation between father and son or, in Jung's paradigm, the unconscious and the conscious. This relation is the function Jung attributes to spirit. But since this function is endemic to man and so universal, Jung points to a Trinitarian pantheism in which the spirit is a residual and natural aspect of the psyche functioning to relate its conscious and unconscious poles in greater configurations of healthy reciprocity. He writes:

> We come inevitably to the conclusion that if the Father appears in the Son and breathes together with the Son, and the Son leaves the Holy Ghost behind for man, then the Holy Ghost breathes in man, too, and thus is the breath common to man, the Son, and the Father.[25]

Jung goes on to present man's experience of the spirit as analogous to the realization that one is engaged in a dialogue with a power greater than the ego, i.e., the unconscious. "Accordingly, the advance to the third stage [of the spirit] means something like a recognition of the unconscious, if not actual subordination to it."[26]

Thus spirit, in that it speaks of a consciousness aware of its relation to its unconscious depths and generative source, is the culmination of the psychic process. This achievement is itself a divine process, since in it the divinity of the unconscious becomes incarnate in consciousness. In this way Jung sees the very process of individuation as the human experience that makes possible and necessary man's experience of God as Trinitarian. This process is the psychic equivalent and experiential basis for man's self-understanding as a participant in the triadic flow of divine life. According to Jung this psychic experience is the basis for the metaphysics of the Trinity:

> Consequently, man's achievement of consciousness appears as the result of prefigurative archetypal processes or—to put it metaphysically—as part of the divine life-process. In other words, God becomes manifest in the human act of reflection.[27]

We have seen Tillich's understanding of the Trinity to rest on a symbolic representation of life made up of opposites functioning in harmonious interrelationship within the Godhead, and ambiguously and fragmentarily in man to the extent his life intersects with its Trinitarian ground. The experience of this intersection gives rise to man's sense of God and of God as Trinity. Jung echoes this position almost exactly:

> The Trinity, therefore, discloses itself as a symbol that comprehends the essence of the divine *and* the human. It is, as Koepgen says, "a revelation not only of God but at the same time of man."[28]

And yet the Christian symbol of the Trinity remains, for Jung, peculiarly incomplete. It lacks its completion in "the fourth," which Jung, from varying viewpoints, identifies with evil and/or the devil, woman, and material creation itself beyond God. All of these elements are linked by their absence in Trinitarian life. Jung's argument is that the Christian symbol of the Trinity is cerebral, ideational, and imbalanced towards the spiritual, and so with distinct affinities to the Platonic trinity which is divested of any grounding in the material. Hence the Christian symbol of the Trinity cannot address man's material, sexual, and instinctive life. Jung proposes that the Trinity be extended to a quaternity, in order to include these missing elements, and that the notion of spirit be enlarged to include not only the opposites of Father and Son but also the opposites of the light and dark sides of both divine and human life—

those opposites symbolized in the split between Christ and the devil in Christian thought.[29]

In this context Jung argues that the unconscious motivation of the medieval alchemists, for the most part believing Christians, was the integration of the darker side of the psyche with their spirituality. Furthermore Jung reveals that, in his experience, the Trinity comes into symbolic preeminence only where the fourth cannot be integrated and must be rejected. Hence his many remarks that one of the legitimate historical functions of original Christianity was to curb excesses in man's instinctuality rampant at that time. Implicit in this is that a movement to a spirituality or conception of Holy Spirit which integrates the missing fourth may be the modern demand of the human spirit.

On the question of the missing fourth and the problem of evil, Tillich's thought can be compared to Jung's with certain interesting parallels. Unlike Jung, Tillich draws a more consistent distinction between an intra-Trinitarian reality within the life of God itself, and an extra-Trinitarian procession into creation. In terms of the Trinity itself, Tillich contends that all created possibility is expressed in its essential perfection by the father in the Logos. But essential perfection within the Godhead remains in a state of "dreaming innocence," meaning that divine ideas, expressed in the divine mind, though they constitute the essential perfection of all that can be, remain somehow unreal unless they are expressed beyond God in existence.

This dynamic, located by Tillich within the Godhead, constitutes an implicit demand within the divine dynamic itself that it express itself beyond itself, in order to complete itself through creation. But as the essential goes forth into existence through the reality of creation, it necessarily falls from the purity of its expression in the intra-Trinitarian Logos.

Thus in existence the essential, and particularly the human essential, is fallen, distorted, and only an ambiguous realization of its divine exemplar. Yet even in existential alienation the essential self remains in dialectical continuity with the divine Logos.

This leads directly to Tillich's understanding of the *privatio boni,* the idea that evil is the privation of good, which Jung terms a blatant evasion of the pervasive reality of evil. Tillich's sense of this doctrine, so odious to Jung, is based on his position that man in existence retains his essential inhesion in the life of God, and so remains indestructibly good in his essence. This essential goodness is diminished in existence by its distance from God and further diminished by man's will, which is always individual but exercised universally to affirm himself in discontinuity and independence from his divine ground, and so to deepen the breach.

Hence man's situation in existence is depicted in the tension between his experience of his essential self and his existential distance and alienation from it. Tillich believes that man cannot destroy the groundedness of his essential being in God, but neither can he regain it or confer it upon himself. The gates of paradise have closed behind him and his recovery of the essential in the depths of his being must come as grace. The movement towards or back to the essential, however, is still the basic movement of life, and the basis in Tillich for his thought on Eros as the movement of the universe and man back to its eternal source.

Whatever their apparent differences, then, Tillich's understanding of the *privatio boni* and the missing fourth is not so far from Jung's thought on individuation as a process of movement towards the self. Jung speaks of this process as one of coming into a fuller or more compendious personality through the progressive integration of the unconscious, but like Tillich he believes that man can neither reject this movement in his life with impunity nor bring it to a definitive completion within a lifetime.

For Jung the self always remains beyond, a lure onwards, and man moving towards it always suffers some privation of its fullness. If he were to identify with the self he would fall into inflation, come to hold some partial completion as total and so abort his fuller growth and balance. If the theological meaning of the *privatio boni* were recast in terms of the impossibility of existential man either evading the demands of, or totally attaining, the essential self, such a perspective could form the basis of a greater rapport between the thought of Tillich and Jung. By extension, it might create a greater rapport between theologies based on this ancient view and modern psychologies sharing Jung's insight into the reality and pervasiveness of evil.

Moreover, Jung's criticism that the Trinity cannot accommodate the fourth (understood as creation and matter) could be alleviated by a theology which located a noncompulsive necessity in the flow of divine life to create beyond itself, as do most theologies of emanation. These theologies have always included in the nature of the divinity itself a demand to create. They also imply that as creation proceeds from its divine matrix, it yet retains a relationship with it, distorted or "evil" to the extent of its distance from that divine source.

Modern variants of this position are to be found in the thought of Hegel and Teilhard de Chardin, both of whom see creation and history as necessary emanations from God destined to return to Him as contributions to His completion. In fact Teilhard contends that a theology of creation which cannot be shown to complete the God-head both devalues creation and cripples human creativity within it.

This theme of an intimacy between creation and God is present in Tillich's thought through its indebtedness to nineteenth-century German romanticism and idealism. In his work on faith Tillich writes that God both knows Himself and prays to Himself through man,[30] a traditionally "mystical" view that denies an autonomous and self-sufficient God, one who arbitrarily authors a material creation (which remains something of a divine afterthought) rather than the medium in which God is present and through which He reveals Himself to man. Such theological models exist within Christianity from pseudo-Dionysius to Teilhard de Chardin. Indeed, there is much evidence that Teilhard felt, with the same intensity as Jung discerns in the alchemists, the spiritually debilitating effect of the removal of the divine from matter by theologies of unqualified transcendence. Teilhard, like Jung, speaks of the need for a return to a certain pantheism within Christianity if it is to again become an energizing force for the human spirit.

From the preceding it is clear that Tillich and Jung share certain basic convictions. Both contend that man's experience of God is grounded in man's interiority and both extend this conviction to man's experience of God as Trinitarian. Here nuanced differences appear, though such differences are not overwhelming or decisive. Tillich understands God as the ground of being to be a God who unites the opposites in Himself and in the lives of those in whom divine power is operative. For Jung the psychic motion of the reunion of the ego with the unconscious is both the work of the Holy Spirit and the basis of man's experience of the Holy Spirit—the goal of the gnostic, the alchemist, and the mystic of all times and places. "The Paraclete descends upon the single individual," writes Jung, "who is thereby drawn into the Trinitarian process."[31] In fact, Jung's description of man's experience of his unity with the flow of Trinitarian life through an emerging connection with the unconscious, and Tillich's description of man's experience of the unification and expansion of his life through being grasped by the ground of his being, refer to the same experience, only from the point of view of two different models.

Tillich calls the triadic flow of life that underlies human life the ground of being. Working as a Christian, systematic theologian out of a philosophical background, Tillich gives an ontological status to this ground of being. By this he means that every human life partici-

pates in the being of the God who grounds it. This radical Trinitarian pantheism lies at the heart of his religious experience and the
theological system he builds upon it. Thus man experiences both the
overwhelming power and supportive expression of the Godhead in
his own life. Both Jung and Tillich refer to Luther's experience of
the ambivalence of this God, and to Luther's fear of the dark
demonic side of the Godhead. But for Tillich this experience provides the experiential or epistemological grounds for his ontological
assertion that the being of the life of God and man intersect in such
a way that the former supports, unifies, and expands the latter, as
man takes God into himself.

Jung too uses the term "ground," with reference to his conception
of the *unus mundus,* that psychic state wherein one's individuality is
experienced as "at one" with the totality—operative for example in
synchronistic phenomena, where events in the outer world coincide
in a meaningful way with what is happening inside. Thus he sees the
alchemical quest as an attempt to effect a union with "a potential
world, the eternal Ground of all empirical being."[32] The experience
of such a unity would be similar to Tillich's description of the unity
of man with the ground of his being. The belief in the possibility of
such an experience, of course, presupposes that in each individual
life there is a connecting point with the totality, understood as that
most fecund unity from which all multiplicity proceeds.

In terms of the logic of Jung's thought he quite understandably
relates the *unus mundus,* or ground of being, to both the mandala
and to synchronicity, as two expressions of that final unity of the
individual with the totality towards which the psyche seems to move.
Jung writes, "If mandala symbolism is the psychological equivalent
of the *unus mundus,* then synchronicity is its parapsychological
equivalent."[33]

The *unus mundus* and the mandala both point to a centre which
relates the individual to the whole; such an image itself implies that
the individual in his depths has access to the all. The *unus mundus*
and synchronicity are related in that the conception of the *unus
mundus* implies an underlying creative unity, including that between
matter and spirit. This underlying unity is in effect an acausal connecting principle, which can manifest as "meaningful coincidence"
not only in the present but across time and space. Tillich is expressing a similar view when he talks about the "eternal now,"[34] an
image consistent with his belief that the being of time and eternity,
man and God, interpenetrate, and that this interpenetration makes
possible man's sense of God.

There remains the question of the level of Jung's discourse. At times he protests that he speaks only as a psychologist and empiricist or phenomenologist, and will not commit himself to statements about what may lie beyond the archetypes and their symbols. Yet in his discussion of the symbol of the Trinity, and elsewhere, he seems to say more. For instance he heartily concurs in the decision of the Church to retain the doctrine of three persons sharing one substance, because in essence he feels the Trinity is a symbol of "the progressive transformation of one and the same substance, namely, the psyche as a whole."[35] He goes on to say that since the Trinity is a symbol of the actualization of the self, then "the self must represent something that is of the substance of the Father too." And again he writes that "through the descent of the Holy Ghost, the self of man enters into a relationship of unity with the substance of God."[36]

Since Jung understands "the descent of the Holy Ghost" to be analogous to, if not identical with, the experience of the unity of ego or son with the unconscious as father, Jung here is actually saying that in the further reaches of the unconscious one touches the reality and power of God. In fact, he observed empirically that modern mandalas put man at their centre, yet do not deny a Supreme Being. "It is clear," he writes, "that in the modern mandala man—the deep ground, as it were, of the self—is not a substitute but a symbol for the deity."[37]

Such statements betray an implicit philosophical position in Jung's psychology. He repeatedly affirms that symbols derived from the archetypes with their attendant numinosity give rise to religious experience. But at times he hints that the archetypes themselves are grounded in something deeper. This is nowhere more powerfully expressed than at the end of his essay on the Trinity:

> These considerations have made me extremely cautious in my approach to the further metaphysical significance that may possibly underlie archetypal statements. There is nothing to stop their ultimate ramifications from penetrating to the very ground of the universe. We alone are the dumb ones if we fail to notice it.[38]

4 The Search for the Nonhistorical Jesus

Both Tillich and Jung showed considerable interest in contemporary understandings of the Christ image. They were concerned that the prevailing interpretations of Christ and the dubious apologies based on them showed no appreciation of the symbolic. In the context of his remark that "the spokesmen of religion have failed to deliver an apologetic suited to the spirit of the age," Jung goes on to say that "a humanization of the Christ-figure coupled with inadequate attempts to write his biography are singularly unimpressive."[1]

This reference to the efforts to write Christ's biography refers to the search for the historical Jesus, based on a literal interpretation of the New Testament. It is a response to the modern need for bare facts, a need indicative of a lost capacity to respond to symbolic literature as such.

Here Tillich's position is again close, at least in spirit, to Jung's. Tillich agrees that whoever the figure may have been who provoked it, history has only the image or picture of the Christ presented by the New Testament. To this picture Tillich attributes a gripping power capable of eliciting the response of faith in those who are grasped by it. Beyond this admitted circularity Tillich feels it impossible and needless to go. Indeed, even to make the effort is to be insensitive to symbolic expression and so to be unable to appreciate or respond to it. It shows a peculiar unawareness that primary religious experience can only be expressed symbolically. It reveals a total misunderstanding of religion, of symbol as its native expression, and of faith as the state of being grasped by the symbol. Hence efforts to go beyond the image of Jesus as the Christ, believes Tillich, reveal more about the mind-set and theological presuppositions of those who make such efforts than they ever can or will about the historical Jesus.[2]

Jung does more than deplore the historical literalism and superficial rationality that attach to modern Christologies. He illustrates the continuity of the Christian myth with "the myths of the Near and Middle East that underlie Christianity,"[3] and shows that even these are expressions of a "universal disposition in man," which he calls the collective unconscious.[4] Thus the Christ is only one personification, admittedly the one that has caught the religious impulse of our aion, of a mythologem or archetypal experience innate to the human psyche. In so extending his understanding of the symbol of Christ, Jung universalizes and consequently relativizes the reality of Christ.

At times Jung speaks harshly of Christianity's claim to uniqueness. "Uniqueness," he writes, "is synonymous with unintelligibility."[5] He feels that theological claims about the uniqueness of Christ have "a disastrous effect on the layman," by taking Christianity out of the field of mythology and, through literalizing it, making it "thoroughly implausible and unworthy of belief."[6] He describes Christianity as "sterilized" by its disconnectedness with those "psychological propensities" in man that would serve, if properly understood, as the basis for a more perceptive understanding and reception of Christianity.[7]

Jung is here objecting to the removal of the Christian myth from its roots in the human, making the gospel foreign, especially to the educated.[8] He counters this kind of theology with a conception of Christ as an archetypal event in which the man behind the image received the projection of those drawn to him, a projection which met deep spiritual needs of that time, needs still relevant today. "Had there not been an affinity—magnet!—between the figure of the Redeemer and certain contents of the unconscious," writes Jung, "the human mind would never have been able to perceive the light shining in Christ and seize upon it so passionately."[9] This affinity or magnet was and is grounded in the unconscious—"the archetype of the God-man" or the "supraordinate totality, the self."[10]

Jung thus argues that the reality of Christ originated in other people, for it is based on a corresponding image in the depths of each and every psyche. In Jung's opinion theologians and preachers would be wise to admit this. "Educated people, for instance, would be much more readily convinced of the meaning of the gospel if it were shown that the myth was always there to a greater or lesser degree, and moreover is actually present in archetypal form in every individual."[11]

Though Jung thus identifies the Christian symbol as an expression of the collective unconscious, he is not happy with the demise of the symbolic sense in general and of the symbol of Christ in particular. He fears its diminution because its loss means that man is effectively cut off from his unconscious and its symbols. The "withering" of the Christian symbol, writes Jung, "is a dangerous development for our psychic health, as we know of no other symbol that better expresses the world of the unconscious."[12] He warns that though Eastern religious symbols "formulate the unconscious just as well as the Christian ones do," they do not bear "the past that is stored up within us."[13] Indeed, caution about too facile an importation or substitution of Eastern symbols for those of Christianity runs throughout Jung's writings on religion. He seems to sum up his own determination to continue to wrestle with the Christian symbols when he writes, "The premise we start from is and remains Christianity, which covers anything from eleven to nineteen centuries of Western life."[14]

Yet Jung's attitude towards the symbol of Christ is not without nuance and critical reserve. Though he feels that the Christ symbol has historically captured and shaped Western religious conscious- ness, and hence cannot be transcended till its full import is inte- grated, he also feels that it is questionable in that it contains no trace of the shadow side of life. The shadow is totally distanced from the symbol of Christ in the symbol of the devil as the personification of evil. In this sense the symbol splits the principles of good and evil. In Jung's view these opposites await an integration in the third, the self as the creation of the spirit. The criticism he makes here is akin to his criticism of the Christian conception of a God in whom there is no darkness. (This is discussed in detail later in this chapter.)

Although Jung has reservations about the absence of a shadow in the figure of Christ, he continues to see it as a symbol of the self. The loss of such a symbol by the collective is therefore very serious. Hence he works to restore the vigour of the symbol, and so of the process of man coming into closer connection with his unconscious in the movement towards a more whole personality.

In Jung's thought on Christ as image of the self, several distinct but unified themes are discernible. He relates the image of Christ as priest and victim to a universal intrapsychic flow of energies, based on the great themes of death and resurrection within the movements of the psyche itself. He relates the image of Christ to the *anthropos* or primordial man, an image of the individual's potential unity with the whole of humanity and human experience. He relates Christ to an inner reality, in terms of man's recapitulating in his own life the relation that is pointed to in Christ's unity with and distance from the father, understood as the creative unconscious. Each of these major motifs is worthy of some discussion, and can serve as the basis of comparison with Tillich's image of Christ as the bearer of New Being.

The controlling focus of Jung's treatment is that of Christ as symbol of the self. Jung is of the opinion that discussion of the Christ image continues to be necessary because, though diminished in power, it continues to be "the still living myth of our culture. He is our culture hero, who, regardless of his historical existence, em- bodies the myth of the Primordial Man, the mystic Adam."[15] Jung places great emphasis on the subjective presence of Christ. "As Christ is in us, so also is his heavenly kingdom."[16] Jung associates this inner presence with man as the image of God and understands this image to have been deformed rather than destroyed in the fall, "and can be restored through God's grace."[17] In this his position is identical with Tillich's. Pursuing this line of thought, Jung contends that the restoration of man to the fullness of his nature is a process of suffering comparable to Christ's descent into hell.[18] Tillich also uses this image to describe the process of atonement or of man's becoming at one with his essential nature. Jung goes on to say that the psychological equivalent of the restoration of the image of God in man "is the integration of the collective unconscious, which forms an essential part of the individuation process."[19]

Jung further relates this reformation of man to an archetypal impulse of the psyche towards wholeness. For this reason symbols of wholeness such as the mandala "cannot in practice be distinguished from a God-image."[20] Thus the Christian is connecting, through Christ, with "an ever-present archetype of wholeness."[21] This process Jung describes as both "the restoration of an original condition,"[22] and as an "anamnesis" in which, "the original state of oneness with the God-image is restored."[23]

Jung sees Christ, then, as a symbol of man made whole and, as whole, imaging God, an ever-present possibility and native tendency in the human psyche. "There can be no doubt," he writes, "that the original Christian conception of the *imago Dei* embodied in Christ meant an all-embracing totality that even includes the animal side of man."[24] Though Jung goes on to criticize the absence of a dark side in the Christ image, his basic understanding of Christ is already evident: Christ is an image of man at one with the totality of his being, encompassing his instincts and his unconscious. Such a man is also in some real sense at one with all of humanity and human experience—which as we shall see Jung brings out in his understanding of Christ as *anthropos*.

Before this aspect of his thought on Christ is addressed, there is a more pressing question. Jung himself raises it: "Is the self a symbol of Christ, or is Christ a symbol of the self?"[25] Jung believes the latter, and in so doing takes the position that the appearance and impact of the historical Jesus is only one instance, though admittedly of immense import for our aion, of the archetype of the self manifesting in a real person. In speaking of the symbols that were quickly attributed to the personal Jesus, he writes:

> In other words, the symbols represent the prototypes of the Christ-figure that were slumbering in man's unconscious and were then called awake by his actual appearance in history and, so to speak, magnetically attracted.[26]

. But a like phenomenon could happen in other cultures, through other outstanding personalities and their histories, and be depicted in myth and symbols proper to their culture and functioning with the same power and impact that the image of Christ has come to have in the West. Hence Jung speaks of Jesus, Mani, Buddha, and Lao-tse as "pillars of the temple of the spirit. I could give none preference over the other."[27] Thus Jung can quite consistently point to the universality of the symbol of Christ and in so doing render it relative, while at the same time deploring its waning power because with its diminution Western man's access to the wholeness offered by the symbol is lost.

Just how seriously Jung takes this loss is indicated in his startling statement that "*the destruction of the God-image is followed by the annulment of the human personality.*"[28] For Jung, what touches the God image touches the self, and the loss in the West of a central symbol for both could lead to man's loss of access to his recreative depths. Once man is thus divested of his own potentially sustaining energies, he becomes easy prey to depersonalizing mass movements of a social or political nature. He becomes the fodder of what Jung calls the "politico-social delusional systems" which have character-ized so much of our century.[29] Or he clings, out of loyalty rather than faith, to a set of symbols from which the life has gone. Jung describes this state as one of "stagnation . . . threatened in the long run with a lethal end."[30]

Jung further develops these themes in his treatment of Christ as priest and victim, and as primordial man or *anthropos,* in his work on transformation symbolism in the Mass. Here again he shows how these motifs are universally grounded in the psyche, and yet become lived experience only for the individual Christian in whose psyche they come alive through the image of Christ. He also emphasizes the need to personally experience the Christ myth rather than escape the potential impact of its demand and promise through a doctrine of vicarious suffering. In so doing he reveals many aspects of his thought on the dialectical relationship between ego and unconscious.

The ego, Jung believes, is a product of the unconscious and in this respect is constantly transcended by it. He describes the uncon-scious here as "of indefinite extent with no assignable limits."[31] In this sense the self "is, so to speak, an unconscious prefiguration of the ego."[32] Thus Jung establishes a certain passivity of the ego in the face of the unconscious and the "more compendious personality" which the unconscious has in store for the ego.[33] "It is not I who create myself," he writes, "rather I happen to myself."[34] And he goes on immediately to relate the ego to the self as a son to the father or as the moved to the mover. However, the precedence of the uncon-scious to the ego does not reduce the ego to a status of subservient determinism, at least it need not. Rather the ego must cooperate with the intent of the unconscious. From this side of the dialectic the newly emerging self is the product of the ego, the son of the ego's

efforts to integrate the unconscious and so bring the self into existence as its child, the *filius philosophorum.*

It is precisely in this reciprocity that Jung grounds the archetypal
reality of Christ, and by extension, of man as priest and victim. To
the extent that the ego is sacrificed to the demands of the emerging
greater self, it is or can be a willing victim to the self, which acts as
priest in the act of sacrifice. But the process of incarnating in the
finite ego also involves a sacrifice on the part of the self, for it passes
"from potentiality to actuality."[35] This dialectic is at the heart of the
process of individuation and is, for Jung, the mystery behind both
the symbolism of the Mass and the image of Christ as priest and
victim. He writes, "What nevertheless drives us to [individuation] is
the self, which demands sacrifice by sacrificing itself to us."[36]

The symbol of the suffering of Christ is therefore a symbol of
what occurs in every life in which the individuation process takes
place. It is the suffering of the ego before the demands of the self
towards balanced growth. But since the self emerges or is born from
the conjunction of the finite ego with an unconscious which is without known limits and so functionally infinite, the movement towards
the self can never end. Jung writes, "Since the growth of personality
comes out of the unconscious, which is by definition unlimited, the
extent of the personality now gradually realizing itself cannot in
practice be limited either."[37]

The consequence is that suffering is inherent in the process of
individuation. The ego must continually die and be reborn to greater
consciousness through the integration of the unconscious.

For these reasons Jung objects to interpreting the suffering of
Christ as the punishment of the innocent for the sins of the guilty.
The suffering of Christ is intrinsically related to the process of
growth towards the self.[38] On the same basis Jung objects to the
conception of vicarious suffering, wherein Christ is understood to
atone for man's sins and so spare the individual the suffering which
he alone can undertake in the process of maturation. In other words,
the *imitatio Christi* has for Jung little relationship to the detailed
reenactment or imitation of an external and past life, that of Jesus.
Rather it refers to the suffering through which each man must go, as
the archetypal events and processes symbolized by the suffering of
Christ are repeated in his personal life and experience.

Through the suffering attached to the development of the self
emerges man's experience, again symbolized in Christ, of himself as
anthropos. This happens through the realization that the centre of
the individual is also "the centre of the universe, and in this wise the
goal of man's salvation and exaltation is reached."[39]

The notion that microcosm and macrocosm are essentially identical is an ancient one which holds, in a variety of historical expressions, that man's interiority is the place of his intersection with the whole.[40] (Tillich expresses the same thing when he indicates that in the ground of his being man relates to all being.) Jung writes, "The unconscious is the universal mediator among men. It is in a sense the all-embracing One, or the one psychic substratum common to all."[41] Jung expresses the idea that unity in depth with oneself is unity with the universe, in dramatic, even startling language:

[Man] is of the same essence as the universe, and his own mid-point is its centre. This inner experience, shared by Gnostics, alchemists, and mystics alike, has to do with the nature of the unconscious—one could even say that it *is* the experience of the unconscious.[42]

In his view of the symbol of Christ as *anthropos,* Jung echoes Tillich's thought on Christ as essential man, and the meaning of the Christian life as a process of becoming essential through the power of that symbol. Both are concerned to show that man's true individuality is grounded in a reality that is at once greater than himself and yet universally present to him. Tillich does this with his understanding of the Logos as the eternal expression of the creative power of the Godhead, and so as the seat of all individuality in its pristine and essential purity. Jung in his understanding of the *anthropos* shares a similar vision, locating the self in the *anthropos* much as Tillich locates the essential self in the Logos. Both mean that the truest being or expression of the individual somehow lies beyond him, but that its realization relates the individual intensely to the totality.

Jung writes, for instance, that "the self is the Anthropos above and beyond this world, and in him is contained the freedom and dignity of the individual man."[42] Moreover, Jung relates the *anthropos* to Christ as the principle of individuation and associates these images with the Logos. His idea is that all individuality proceeds from the matrix of the unconscious, and must reintegrate itself with its matrix in a maturation that achieves an individuality in resonance with all that is. Jung felt that such insights were more proper to gnosticism and suggests that such a religious perspective "could serve many people today as a bridge to a more living appreciation of Christian tradition."[43] There is a note both winsome and true in that remark. Perhaps Tillich's theology itself contributes to the bridge between the current state of Christian religiosity and the liveliness it might regain with a more gnostic spirit, for he is quite explicit in searching out and describing the nature of a true Christian gnosis.

In summary, then, Jung understands Christ as a symbol of the self and so as a symbol of the direction in which universal psychic life moves, namely, towards that wholeness which results from the deepening marriage of ego and unconscious. This process is itself one of suffering. Its rhythm is naturally one of continuous death and resurrection, as the ego cedes to the growth induced by the unconscious and as the unconscious accepts the constrictions of incarnation in the finitude of consciousness. This suffering must be borne by each individual. It cannot be vicariously performed by some past historical figure. Yet as this process continues it relates the individual to humanity, to his potential coincidence with human experience in all its breadth. This experience is the substance which gives birth to and is captured in the symbol of the *anthropos,* the original or primordial man.

Given this orientation Jung naturally emphasizes the necessity of the Christ experience in the depth of each life. He speaks frequently of the need to regain the sense of the "inner Christ" or "the Christ within."[44] And here he frankly acknowledges the dangers attendant to such a spirituality. For the experience of the inner Christ could lead to an identification of the ego with it, that is, to an inflation in which the ego would be possessed by and lost to the image of Christ.[45] For these reasons Jung acknowledges some wisdom in the Church's efforts to portray Christ as an external, distant, and historical reality.[46] But while he cautions against the danger of inflation, he insists that the symbolic reality of Christ is "an inner psychic fact" or "a psychic centre in all," and that the search for and experience of this Christ lie at the heart of the Western gnostic, alchemical, and Christian mystical traditions.[47]

In describing the experience of the inner Christ, Jung speaks of a power greater than the ego grasping it, rather than the ego grasping this power. Similarly, Tillich frequently speaks of the experience of faith in terms of being grasped by the object of one's faith rather than grasping it. Jung echoes this in psychological terms: "[Man] cannot conquer the tremendous polarity of his nature on his own resources; he can only do so through the terrifying experience of a psychic process that is independent of him, that works *him* rather than he *it*."[48] This process would be the inbreaking power of the unconscious in the interests of the self, symbolized in Western tradition by the Christ figure.

Translated into theological terms, Jung is saying that the ego is not the author of its own redemption or wholeness. Rather this healing is experienced as coming from a power greater than itself. The consequence of such conversion, or indeed the substance of it, is a state of psychic integration which Jung closely relates to grace. He describes this state as "the original feeling of unity, which was integrally connected with the unity of the unconscious psyche."[49] The absence of this unity Jung describes as a fragmented consciousness in which reality is "broken down into countless particulars."[50] In this condition the fragments (or complexes) take over the personality, which appears as neurotic one-sidedness. When it happens collectively or socially, society is removed from its sense of unity with nature and its members are alienated from, and aggressive towards, each other.

Tillich too deplores man's distance from his underlying continuity with nature. Sometimes he calls this the Logos. Sometimes he calls it the depths of reason. Alienation from either, in individual or society, is inevitably accompanied by shallowness, superficiality, and a debilitating loss of substance and meaning. Like Jung, Tillich feels that this loss alienates man from the very possibility of potential communion with his fellowmen and nature. Thus the price of a collective consciousness reduced to technical reason, for instance, is the reduction of man and his relationships to the level of means to be manipulated towards ends.

*

Though Jung and Tillich give fresh vitality to the symbol of Christ by showing its universal and holistic aspects, Jung had, as already mentioned, serious reservations about it. Just as he feels that the Christian conception of God denies His dark, irrational side, so he also feels that the symbol of Christ does not account for the dark side of the self, the dark side that must be assimilated in the process of individuation.

Jung's thought on the absence of any shadow qualities in the figure of Christ closely relates to his thinking on the development of the conception of God from the Old to the New Testaments. As such it contains an implicit theory of the development of religious consciousness itself. In Jung's view the God of the Old Testament, Yaweh, was a God of moral ambivalence lacking in moral differentiation, a God with whom Satan could remain on good terms. Jung points to this moral ambivalence most explicitly in his essay "Answer to Job."[51] Here he illustrates that there was a "dual aspect" in the undifferentiated God of the Old Testament, but when this God became incarnate, and so defined in man, His incarnation itself forced the moral differentiation into the wholly good in Christ, and the wholly evil in Satan. Jung writes, "But the real devil first appears as the adversary of Christ, and with him we gaze for the first time into the luminous realm of divinity on the one hand and into the abyss of hell on the other."[52]

Jung goes on to show both the gain and the pain of such differentiation. Its gain was to give to man a sharp awareness of the split between good and evil. Jung willingly concedes that without this split, "human consciousness could hardly have progressed so far as it has towards mental and spiritual differentiation."[53] The pain attached to such progress is that man is now suspended on the cross between the opposites, symbolized in the manner of Christ's death.[54] Out of such sustained moral suffering maturation develops, often led on by the symbol that can integrate or unite the apparently irreconcilable opposites. Thus Jung's understanding of the problematic side of Christ, his unalloyed goodness, is dialectical. Christ as a personification of the light side of the Godhead brings to consciousness the problem of the integration of the dark side.

Jung seeks a solution to this dilemma in the Spirit as uniting the split in the moral opposites symbolized by Christ and Satan. The Spirit is the fourth, bringing together the opposite sons of the Father, Christ and Satan. "Looked at from a quaternary standpoint," writes Jung, "the Holy Ghost is a reconciliation of opposites and hence the answer to the suffering in the Godhead which Christ personifies."[55] Thus for Jung the Spirit unites the exclusively spiritual reality of Christ with that which is identified with the devil, including "the dark world of nature-bound man," the chthonic side of human nature excluded by Christianity from the Christ image.[56]

It is in the effort to bring about this synthesis that Jung locates much of the meaning of alchemy. The alchemists sought to reconcile their spiritual reality with the darker side of their nature, to redeem "the fallen Lucifer" and to experience in their lives the *anima mundi* hidden in matter.[57] Their aim was to release the spirit from matter and in so doing elevate the material to the spiritual. In psychological terms, the alchemist seeks God in the matter of unconsciousness, and in making Him conscious becomes the occasion of His incarnation and completion. And here again Jung is very aware that, because such experience can give to man a sense of his own divinity, it is fraught with the danger of inflation—though this very possibility presupposes that man possesses in himself a germ of divinity.[58]

For these reasons Jung understands the alchemical figure of Mercurius to be a compensation for the one-sidedness of the symbol of Christ.[59] He relates Mercurius to both the *anthropos*[60] and the *anima mundi,* as well as to the *lumen naturae,*[61] by which Jung means the light in man which is natural, as opposed to the supernatural light of revelation and ecclesiastical mediation. Jung further connects Mercurius with the fire of God burning in the Godhead and in man.[62] In comparison with Christ he is "ambiguous, dark, paradoxical, and thoroughly pagan."[63] As Christ is the archetype of consciousness, so is Mercurius the archetype of the unconscious. As binary opposites they exist in a state of tension: Mercurius is the earthy spiritual complement to the ungrounded spirituality that attaches to the image of Christ.

In Jung's view the full implications and power of the symbols of the *anthropos* and Mercurius are a threat to the Church because they "mean" that the experience of the Spirit is directly accessible. Yet precisely because this experience is not currently and powerfully mediated by ecclesial authorities, the Christian, in Jung's opinion, too often stands "in need of a doctor," in order to connect with his instinctual roots.[64] To this distortion of the Spirit away from the bodily and the instinctual, Jung feels the image of Christ as unmitigated good and light has made a significant contribution.

A variant of this same problem arises in Jung's discussion of Paracelsus' thought. How does the natural light in matter and the soul relate to the supernatural light of revelation? Jung understands Paracelsus to mean that the natural light is very closely related to the light of the Holy Spirit, and that it emanates from within man in contrast to the light received from a transcendent God and mediated through the Church. Jung agrees with this position, similar to that of the alchemists. Those in whom the light of nature is activated come into an unmediated and so direct experience of the ultimate, at once both human and divine: "The light that is lighted in the heart by the grace of the Holy Spirit, that same light of nature, however feeble it may be, is more important to them than the great light which shines in the darkness and the darkness comprehended not."[65]

This light, in effect, would be that of the *anthropos* immanent in nature, the soul of the world, the mercurial spirit. Just how the heavenly and chthonic trinities, the spirit of Christ and the spirit of Mercurius, the natural and the supernatural lights, are to be united is a central issue in Jung's thought. Obviously the union of these opposites would constitute the ultimate psychological and, by extension, theological and spiritual goal. The dilemma centres around Jung's realization that Christianity has constellated the opposites of absolute moral good in conflict with absolute moral evil. In doing this it has freed the soul from enslavement to the instinctual but at the risk of alienating man from a large part of his nature.

In his later work, *Mysterium Coniunctionis,* Jung's thought on this problem reaches a certain culmination and clarity. Here he suggests that the soul, once freed from the bodily and instinctual life through its union with the spirit, must be reincarnated in a second conjunction. Only then can the experience of unity with the whole, the *unus mundus,* take place. Such an experience would be characterized by a sense of "at oneness" or atonement, and the realization that the bodily and spiritual complement rather than contradict each other.

*

Passing now to Tillich's understanding of the Christ image, we find an emphasis on essence and existence, and how these concepts function in the human situation. Basically, Tillich understands the essential to be equated with the good because the essential ultimately resides in the divine, both within and beyond creation. In particular, the essential as principle of structure and individuation resides in the second principle of the divine life, the Logos, which is the expression and definition of God's power, containing in its eternal form all that can be expressed beyond the Godhead in creation and time.

In this conceptual framework the original and continuing event of creation itself can be defined in terms of "the transition from essence to existence."[66] Existence refers to the process of the departure of essential reality from its basis in God, and so to its separation or fall from its divine expression in the Logos. In this dialectical process the realities of creation and fall coincide:

> If God creates here and now, everything he has created participates in the transition from essence to existence. He creates the new born child; but, if created, it falls into the state of existential estrangement.[67]

In this passage Tillich describes man's plight viewed, as it were, from the side of God. From the other side, in more psychological terms, he speaks of man in a state of "dreaming innocence,"[68] a condition which is really one of unactualized potential—a state of innocent but immature unity with God preceding self-consciousness and willful self-affirmation. As man becomes conscious he loses his dreaming state of innocence, he begins "to exist." In so doing he removes himself from unambiguous, though preconscious, unity with his source in God. Thus man in some real and universal sense is torn between a unity with God in which his human potential is not actualized, and the actualization of this potentiality in existence— with the consequent break from God.

For Tillich this describes the dynamics of temptation. The temptation is to actualize oneself, which Tillich believes most individuals do; they come into existence, but at the cost of unambiguous unity with their groundedness in God. And so man's tragic situation centres on the contradiction that in "standing out" (the meaning of existence Tillich derives from the Latin verb *exsto,* to stand out of) of his divine potential, he is involved inevitably but freely in the fall from his essence.

With this use of the categories of essence and existence, Tillich combines the traditional themes of original and personal sin. The scenario he describes points to a universal situation wherein man in actualizing himself falls from a unity with the divine. Because man wills himself and his actualization he is personally responsible. However, in Tillich's thought, the essential never deserts man in his existential predicament. Or to put it the other way around, man never totally divests himself of some residual and ontological participation in the essential, the ground of his being. On the contrary, it is man's experienced retention of his relation to the essential that makes him aware of the pain and wrongness of his existential estrangement, and drives him in the search of possible redemption. Thus the sense of sin and the search for redemption are states of consciousness that Tillich ascribes to man's memory of his original, essential unity. The recovery of this state is then the inner meaning and direction of human life, personal and collective.

Tillich's understanding of man's drive towards essence from a condition of existential alienation is comparable to Jung's view of the movement of the psyche towards the self, as towards the completion or wholeness of the personality. Jung sees the ego's emergence from the unconscious as a certain primary maturation process in the attainment of relative autonomy from its generative source. This initial self-affirmation or self-possession involves a fall and a certain amount of tension. Yet the break from the unconscious is never so total that the ego does not seek reunion with it as the source of renewal, balance, and expansion.

Again in terms that have an obvious psychological flavour, Tillich shows how man in existential estrangement from his essence undergoes a process of disintegration. He explicitly relates this to psychopathology and to the "horrifying experience of 'falling to pieces.'"[69] Here Tillich is in remarkable accord with the spirit of Jung's remark that the loss of the image of God in man is followed by a loss of personality. Their common assumption is that life, whether divine or human, is made up of polar opposites in a state of tension. To break the relationship is to negate the function of spirit and to destroy life. To foster the relationship is to create spirit and life.

With this in mind, it is clear that for Tillich the central meaning of the symbol of Christ is the reuniting of the individual with his or her essential self. Hence he designates Christ or the experience of Christ as New Being, a term that is itself highly symbolic, pointing to the experiential recovery of the essential self.

It is under his conception of Christ as the personification of essential humanity that Tillich deals with the question of grace. Man in existence cannot himself attain his longed-for essence. Tillich is quite adamant about this, affirming that both the reality of Christ and man's transformation under the impact of Christ are experienced as gift and as grace. On this point Tillich and Jung speak virtually the same language. Jung, for instance, in describing the alchemist's efforts to integrate the unconscious and so, in effect, redeem himself, notes that the alchemist always attached the qualifier *Deo concedente* ("God willing") to the success of his work. Jung does seem to consider in certain of his statements that the alchemist's effort is one of self-salvation and is, therefore, heretical in relation to the Christian doctrine of grace. However, in other passages he describes the unconscious as autonomous and, in a very real sense, transcendent to the position of the ego within the psyche. As such it is a power that grips the ego just as Tillich's New Being grasps rather than is grasped by the believer. In other words, the ego may cooperate with the source of redemption—whether it be called Christ or the unconscious—but can never coerce it.

Tillich supposes that man as a seeker of his essential humanity is the bearer of "the universal human expectation of a new reality."[70] For the Christian, this reality appears in history in the life that lies behind and gave rise to the symbol of the Christ. "The paradox of the Christian message," writes Tillich, "is that in *one* personal life essential manhood has appeared under the conditions of existence without being conquered by them."[71] He does admit that the attribution of essential humanity exclusively to the figure of Christ is an act of his Christian faith and involves a certain circularity. Yet he is able to give a rather convincing philosophical understanding of the reality of Christ as the fullest realization of humanity at one with its divine ground. "One could also speak of essential God-manhood," writes Tillich, "in order to indicate the divine presence in essential manhood; but this is redundant, and the clarity of thought is served best in speaking simply of essential manhood."[72] This implies that humanity in its essence is divine, and that the realization of this humanity by Christ is his basic religious significance.

Tillich also illustrates in the context of his Christology that the search for the essential self is both religious and universal. This parallels Jung's contention that individuation is a religious process. Jung insists that this process only takes place in an individual fully participating in all aspects of life, personal and social. Tillich too feels that authentic spirituality through Christ does not lead out of the day-to-day demands of historical existence. Rather, he writes, "the individual enters a new reality which embraces society and nature."[73]

On the significant question of how the New Being which appeared in Christ is related to the rest of humanity, Tillich believes that the very fact of its having been realized in one life process makes it possible that it appear in others. "If there were no personal life in which existential estrangement had been overcome," he writes, "the New Being would have remained a quest and an expectation and would not be a reality in time and space."[74] Tillich's thinking here is possibly indebted to the microcosm-macrocosm dialectic already seen in Jung's thought. He seems to be saying that what happens in one life process, especially an event of such significance, touches all. He writes, "Only if the existence is conquered in *one* point—a personal life, representing existence as a whole—is it conquered in principle, which means 'in beginning and in power.'"[75]

With the basic meaning of Christ established as essential manhood, Tillich looks at the various symbols applied to Christ in the New Testament. He is aware that they are older than Christ. Thus he relates the symbol "Son of Man" to "the Persian symbol of the Original Man."[76] He understands this to refer to an original unity between God and man from which man has fallen into estrangement, and that from this estrangement he seeks redemption. Tillich understands Christ to apply the term to himself and in so doing to define himself in symbols older than himself. This is quite compatible with Jung's understanding of the *anthropos* symbol as applied to Christ. For both it means the unity of the individual with the totality of himself and of humanity.

For Tillich the Christian is one who has experienced the New Being, essential humanity, in his own life. This experience Tillich identifies with faith. "Faith itself is the immediate . . . evidence of the New Being within and under the conditions of existence."[77] This is not to deny, however, that essential humanity can be realized by non-Christians. The New Being is operative beyond the boundaries of the visible Church, and Tillich also suggests that not all those within the visible Church have experienced the New Being. But Tillich does mean that those who experience their essential humanity experience what the Christian experiences in Christ. For the Christian the power of this New Being is conveyed through "the picture" of Christ in the New Testament. In an argument that is patently circular Tillich claims that "through this picture the New Being has the power to transform those who are transformed by it."[78] In an even more powerful statement he contends that "it was this picture which created both the church and the Christian."[79] Here he pays frank tribute to the symbol of Christ as having the power to grip, and to elicit the faith response which has been the basis of the collective Western religion for two millen-

ia. Most significantly, for Tillich, the realization of essential manhood in Christ makes it possible for everyone after this event to
participate in it, however ambiguously.

When he gives content or substance to what such participation
might mean, Tillich speaks of healing and centredness. Indeed, he
tends to interpret salvation substantially as healing in depth, in
which man is united with his divine ground and so with God, man,
and nature. In this sense Christ as the bringer of New Being re-
stores man to himself by reestablishing his centredness in God:

> Healing means reuniting that which is estranged, giving a center to
> what is split, overcoming the split between God and man, man and
> his world, man and himself. Out of this interpretation of salvation,
> the concept of the New Being has grown.[80]

Again these words correlate closely with Jung's understanding of
psychic health as ultimately involving the reconnection of the individual with a reality beyond himself, as symbolized by the *anthropos*.

Tillich is very sensitive to the difference between Christ and the
Christian, and so to the fact that this depth healing is never completely realized. This echoes Jung's belief that the process of individuation, the movement towards the self, is endless, since the unconscious is inexhaustible. In other words, the healing power of the
New Being, manifest and operative in a dramatic way in the event
and symbol of Christ, is both universal and relative:

> In some degree all men participate in the healing power of the New
> Being. Otherwise, they would have no being. The self-destructive
> consequences of estrangement would have destroyed them. But no
> men are totally healed, not even those who have encountered the
> healing power as it appears in Jesus as the Christ.[81]

One sees how intimately Tillich connects God's power to unite
opposites with Christ's meaning as the bearer of the New Being.
Christ is the symbol of God's creating and sustaining power which
holds together the opposites that make up life. Were not a certain
unifying power of God at work universally, man and creation
would disintegrate. For Tillich the power of God as it works
through Christ is specifically the power of integration and this integration is the depth meaning of healing. This follows directly from
Tillich's view of life as made up of opposites in tension, continually
threatened with the loss of their centre and so with splitting into
unrelated opposites. In this sense annihilation, both psychic and
spritual, is the consequence of the loss of centredness.

Jung does not use such ontological language but he too sees the
unification of the personality as dependent on a centre or self,
which knits together the disparate parts of the psyche, and does so

on a universal basis. Like Tillich, he also sees wholeness as relative. Where such integration is seriously absent, Jung refers to the disintegration of the personality in terms of neurosis or psychosis. Thus both Tillich and Jung point to a power operative in life which holds together its contending opposites and in so doing makes life first possible and then richer. Tillich calls this power the New Being and relates it to Christ. Jung calls it the self, of which Christ is the most powerful symbol in Western religious consciousness. Both attribute a religious connotation to the process of becoming whole and see this process as the substance of salvation.

Jung's dismissal of the conception of vicarious suffering has already been mentioned. He feels the Christian must experience in his own life the realities of death and resurrection symbolized in Christ's. Tillich, too, is hostile to ideas of substitutional atonement which do not engage the experience of the believer: "The doctrine of atonement is the description of the effect of the New Being in Jesus as the Christ on those who are grasped by it in their state of estrangement."[82]

Thus atonement is one aspect of the experience in a personal life process of the New Being of Christ, and in particular that aspect which describes the suffering involved in coming into one's essential humanity. This suffering Tillich likens to what happens in depth therapy, "with its practice of making the patient go through the torment of existential insight into his being... before promising any healing."[83]

Tillich goes on to ground his understanding of atonement on God's suffering participation in creation and man's participation in this suffering. Ultimately Tillich explains this in terms of the living God who conquers all negativity within himself as Trinity and, as the ground of being of creation, struggles there to overcome negativity by leading creation back to the balanced and yet inexhaustible life of its divine matrix. This participation of God in the suffering of the world is, for Tillich, the meaning of Christ's cross.[84]

Jung, speaking rather more symbolically, is also very sensitive to the theme of the suffering participation of the Godhead in creation. In the process of becoming whole, both the ego and the source of its being in the unconscious enter into a mutual suffering. "The whole world is God's suffering," writes Jung, "and every individual man who wants to get anywhere near his own wholeness knows that this is the way of the cross."[85]

In summary, it must be said that both Tillich and Jung interpret the reality of Christ using categories that transcend those of explicitly Christian dogma. In this endeavour they are involved in a form of natural theology whose traditional task has been to mediate the meaning of Christ in terms not taken from Christian revelation. The only other option is some from of fundamentalism, often working hand in hand with literal interpretation. They also seek to reveal the meaning of Christ first of all to the Christian, as the primary task of a modern apology. And both are concerned to show that man is religious by nature, and that the process of becoming human is itself religious.

Tillich does this by showing that man's drive to become essential is the ultimate motivation of both personal and historical life. For Tillich, Christ meets this drive in man, and through the impact of the symbol man experientially participates in the essential humanity of Christ. For Jung, the drive to individuation is the empowering *telos* of life, a holy task moving towards a condition of wholeness in which man rediscovers his nature as image of God. Both reject theories of vicarious satisfaction which would relieve the Christian of the personal experience of the heights and depths of this task, for only in the experience of one's own suffering, and repeated death and resurrection in the service of the self, does the individual experience in his life the substance of the Christ event.

What separates Jung and Tillich is Jung's insistence on the one-sidedness of the Christ image. Jung's criticism is basically that the image of Christ has no shadow, or that his shadow is split from him in the symbol of the devil. Tillich comes closest to facing this question in his treatment of the temptation of Christ, suggesting that though Christ was free to submit to these temptations yet it was his destiny not to and so to preserve intact his unity with God in existence. This is one aspect of realizing essential manhood in the concrete existence of a personal life history. Questions as to how the Christian is to integrate the dark or evil side, or avoid projecting it onto others, who then become personal or collective demons, are not addressed by Tillich and yet are never far from Jung's mind.

Finally, however, the two are in broad agreement that the symbol of Christ is one which fosters man's unity with the source of his being. It contributes to man's wholeness by bringing together the opposites, and in this capacity it functions in a manner similar to spirit.

5   Aspects of the Spirit

Spirit is commonly understood as the principle of continuity in time with the reality of Christ. The basic link here between Tillich and Jung is that both understand spirit, or the Holy Spirit, as a power which unites opposites. For Tillich the reconciled opposites are primarily power and meaning; for Jung they are, in the broadest terms, consciousness and the unconscious.

Jung especially is sensitive to the ambiguity of the term and its wealth of meanings:

> The same verbal sign, spirit, is used for an inexpressible, transcendental idea of all-embracing significance; in a more commonplace sense it is synonymous with 'mind'; it may connote courage, liveliness, or wit, or it may mean a ghost; it can also represent an unconscious complex. ... In a metaphorical sense it may refer to the dominant attitude in a particular social group—the 'spirit' that prevails there. Finally, it is used in a material sense, as spirits of wine, spirits of ammonia, and spirituous liquors in general.[1]

Elsewhere he notes that spirit can mean simply "God" as opposed to all that is not God.[2] But he also contrasts spirit with nature, matter, and instinct.[3] When its meaning "is restricted to the supernatural or anti-natural," writes Jung, then the concept loses "its substantial connection with psyche and life."[4] When this is done theologically it means that the reality of God is removed from life. Jung himself favours a conception of spirit which is neither separate from nor reducible to the material.

In accordance with this view of spirit as integral to life, Jung points out that in primitive times spirit was experienced as external to man, whereas historically the trend has been towards locating it "in man's consciousness."[5] Jung is concerned not so much to oppose this trend as to remind man of the origin and autonomous power of the spirit, which approaches consciousness from a depth beyond it.[6] Jung's point here is that though modern man may be becoming more conscious of the immanence of spirit he must never lose sight of its overwhelming power relative to ego consciousness. Even when deprived of an external and transcendent origin, spirit retains its power to possess man rather than be possessed by him, and when man is possessed he enters into a dangerous state of inflation and one-sidedness.

Besides the many meanings the term can have, Jung is also aware of an ambivalence or duality within the function of the spirit itself. The spirit can be dark as well as light, of the devil as well as of the divine. Here Jung sounds a theme that runs throughout his work: the need for man to face and to integrate the essential ambivalence of life if he is to be whole.

In Jung's view spirit is closely related to man's experience of the archetypes and so of the unconscious acting to complement, to guide, and to expand one's conscious viewpoint. Hence he relates spirit to an autonomous complex bearing a higher consciousness. He writes that "the phenomenon of spirit, like every autonomous complex, appears as an intention of the unconscious superior to, or at least on a par with, the intentions of the ego."[7] This higher consciousness acts on the ego to expand it or to make it "wider"[8]—by which Jung means it leads the ego into touch with sides of the psyche that have yet to be integrated—but often at the cost of violent conflict with "accepted ideals."[9] In other words, experience of the spirit tends to lead one away from collective values.

The spirit is also endowed with the power to grip, so that the person influenced by it feels moved to act in accord with it. It is thus accompanied by emotion. Jung describes spirit in this sense as the "image of a personified affect."[10] Pursuing this theme Jung contends that the experience of the spirit, as of the unconscious, can only be expressed by the symbol because it is so laden with meaning and hence with mystery. It is an experience which "is darkly divined yet still beyond our grasp," and yet "contains the seeds of incalculable possibilities."[11]

Relying on his knowledge of primitive psychology Jung distinguishes between "soul complexes" and "spirit complexes."[12] The former "belong" to the individual. The individual is impoverished by their loss and enriched by their return and by the ability to use or own the energy attached to them.[13] The spirit complexes, on the other hand, do not belong to the ego, and, if they become associated with it, must be separated from it. Soul complexes reside in the personal unconscious. Spirit complexes reside in the collective unconscious; as such they have a much greater power or fascination and are more foreign to consciousness.[14] Should the ego surrender its authority to them or be overridden by them, a destructive inflation can result. Thus Jung identifies spirits as "complexes of the collective unconscious"; they are activated in personal life when the ego loses its adaptation to reality, and in collective life when the attitude of the society must change.[15] In this sense the benign work of the spirit is to lead the ego, personal or societal, into a more adequate position. The destructive side manifests in personal or collective possession by one or other of the "spirits."

As complexes that originate in the collective unconscious, spirits share in the ambivalence of the archetypes themselves. When they appear in consciousness, the ego must not only preserve its integrity and standpoint in the face of their compelling power, it must also be aware that however good they may appear they invariably carry with them a dark side.

Jung addresses this ambivalence of spirit in related but differing ways. Most obviously, spirit can be destructive to the psyche if it captures the ego and leads it into one-sidedness, so that the individual thus possessed is no longer able to partake in a free life related to other dimensions of spirit. Jung describes this situation when he writes: "There are all too many cases of men so possessed by a spirit that the man does not live any more but only the spirit, and in a way that does not bring him a richer and fuller life but only cripples him."[16] Spirit can work in this destructive manner also on the collective level, producing various "isms" with the power to swamp minds. Jung regrets that such powerful but one-sided truths are often proposed by religious leaders themselves:

> The ego keeps its integrity only if it does not identify with one of the opposites, and if it understands how to hold the balance between them. This is possible only if it remains conscious of both at once. However, the necessary insight is made exceedingly difficult not by one's social and political leaders alone, but also by one's religious mentors. They all want decision in favour of one thing, and therefore the utter identification of the individual with a necessarily one-sided 'truth.'[17]

Even great truths, when they totally possess an individual or nation, are crippling in that they prevent balance and "arrest further spiritual development."[18]

Jung not only cautions against the potentially enslaving power of spirit, he also points up the necessity of integrating its dark side lest it be unleashed with disastrous consequences. Indeed, he frequently relates the rise of National Socialism in Germany to an outbreak of the spirit of Wotan which possessed the nation.[19] He makes it quite clear that the process of "spiritual development" is one in which the ego relates to the archetypal while yet preserving its own authority, and this involves becoming aware of the dark side of the unconscious and assimilating it. "It is possible for a man to attain totality, to become whole," writes Jung, "only with the co-operation of the spirit of darkness, [which is] actually a *causa instrumentalis* of redemption and individuation."[20]

Jung also warns that he should not be read in a reductionist manner. Because he locates the spirits of good and evil in man, he by no means feels that he has reduced their power or reality. On the contrary, he challenges modern man to become aware of these trans-personal powers in his own psyche. He laments the fact that the modern is "abysmally unconscious of the demonism that still clings to him."[21] He challenges man to recognize that the spirit can work for good or evil and that man must become aware of this in himself. Not to do so is the greatest sin. "Man's worst sin is unconsciousness," writes Jung, "but it is indulged in with the greatest piety even by those who should serve mankind as teachers and examples."[22]

In Jung's view, the process of becoming conscious centres around the effort to unite the opposites. The main opposites are those of spirit, by which he means man's "higher aspirations," and nature or instinct, which Jung closely relates to man's physical being. The conflict between them, sometimes described by Jung as the source of all psychic energy, he ascribes to the structure of the psyche itself, based on the polar opposites of instinct and archetype.[23] Hence the tension between instinct and spirit is present from the very beginning, inherent in human nature. Speaking of the psychic process in children Jung states that "in the child-psyche the natural condition is already opposed by a 'spiritual' one," which affirms itself against the natural "with incredible strength."[24]

The movement in the psyche between instinct and archetype (or nature and spirit) is compared by Jung to the variations within the colour spectrum, from infra-red to ultra-violet:

> At one moment [consciousness] finds itself in the vicinity of instinct, and falls under its influence; at another, it slides along to the other end where spirit predominates and even assimilates the instinctual processes most opposed to it.[25]

Jung locates the purely instinctual at the infra-red end of the spectrum and the archetypal image at the ultra-violet end, the area of the spirit. He points out that although blue would seem to be a more appropriate colour for spirit, ultra-violet is in fact a better representation because it is made up of red and blue, and so indicates that "true" spirit is an integration of pure spirit, blue, with the red of instinctuality. He adds that the integration of the instinctual never occurs at the level of instinct, the red end itself, "but only through integration of the image which signifies and at the same time evokes the instinct."[26]

Jung's extensive analogy between psychic processes and the colour spectrum enables him to illustrate in a unique though complex way just what he means by spirit and the spiritual: The truly spiritual would be a conjunction or synthesis of pure spirit and pure instinct so that the spirit would be grounded and instinct spiritualized. Thus the spirit both effects and rises out of the coming together of the wholly spiritual and the wholly instinctual. If either of these opposites dominates, then man's humanity is adversely affected. If an unearthed spirit were to triumph man would be possessed by a one-sided spirituality which could take him out of his body, manifesting as some form of "ism" or fanatical behaviour. If the instincts were to dominate, man would become little more than a beast.

In the sense, then, that the psyche moves to integrate the spiritual and the instinctual in the archetypal symbol, its movement can be called a movement towards spirit: "Psychologically . . . the archetype as an image of instinct is a spiritual goal toward which the whole nature of man strives."[27] Thus Jung speaks of a *spiritus rector* within the psyche, a power superior to the ego which rectifies or balances consciousness by bringing to its aid the needed compensation from the unconscious. In particular he refers to this power as working against the merely intellectual approach to life, for the *spiritus rector* possesses a broader perspective than "intellect and science."[28] It is a guiding force that bears in mind "the claims of a fuller life," and offers to man "a greater guarantee of psychological universality than the intellect alone can compass."[29] The *spiritus rector* works to reconcile the opposites in life, and especially, in modern times, the opposites of scientific thought and human feeling. Such a condition of wholeness can be imaged in the symbol of the child, "that final goal which unites the opposites."[30]

These descriptions of the spirit as "rectifying" the intellect or mind depict the archetypes and the unconscious as constantly proferring to consciousness its complementary needs, in the interests of completion or wholeness. In this sense the *spiritus rector* is in effect an aspect of the self, which works both to balance and expand consciousness through the integration of the unconscious, and yet is somehow a product of this balance. Thus Jung refers to the conscious cooperation in the synthesis of consciousness and the unconscious, elsewhere termed the individuation process, as a "spiritual effort."[31]

*

In one of his latest and greatest works, *Mysterium Coniunctionis,* Jung makes some of his profoundest statements about the unities worked through the spirit and about the totalities into which it leads. He again refers to man's participation in the Trinity, describing such sought-after participation as the goal of the alchemical search, and again identifies the experience of wholeness as the work of the spirit. But in this work he elaborates and endorses a tripartite division in man, consisting of body, soul, and spirit—categories he finds in the writings of Gerhard Dorn, a mediaeval alchemist. In this framework the spirit is a sort of "window into eternity," the soul is an organ of the spirit, and the body an instrument of the soul.[32]

In the process of the developmental unification of the psyche three conjunctions are to take place. First the soul is separated from the body and united with the spirit. This conjunction is called the *unio mentalis* or mental union. It is or can be a stage of ascetic, introverted withdrawal from the distractions of "the turbulent sphere of the body."[33] In alchemical literature it is sometimes likened to death. Jung relates it to the psychological process of coming to terms with the shadow,[34] which results in "an extension of consciousness and the governance of the soul's motions by the spirit of truth."[35] In Jung's opinion it was to this stage that Christinaity led, and it remains Christianity's legitimate and substantial contribution to the development of human spirituality.[36]

The second conjunction is that of the unity of spirit and soul with the body, so that the spirituality of the first conjunction may be grounded in full and bodily participation in life.[37] The third and final conjunction is that of the spiritual body with the totality, symbolized by the expression *unus mundus*. For Jung this symbol points to a creative source or unified centre which underlies and gives rise to all multiplicity. It may be mentioned, incidentally, that Jung views the symbol of the Assumption of Mary as pointing to this unity of the spiritualized soul with the body, and through the body with the totality:

> But a consummation of the *mysterium coniunctionis* can be expected only when the unity of spirit, soul, and body is made one with the original *unus mundus*. This third stage of the coniunctio was depicted [in alchemy] after the manner of an Assumption and Coronation of Mary, in which the Mother of God represents the body.[38]

This universal ground from which individual consciousness derives, and towards which it moves for completion, provides the basis for Jung's thought on synchronicity, that principle of meaningful interaction between individual consciousness and the universe, across the limitations of time and space. "If mandala symbolism is the psychological equivalent of the *unus mundus*," writes Jung, "then synchronicity is its parapsychological equivalent."[39]

In Tillich's system, the Logos as the principle of structure grounded in God functions as the *unus mundus* does in Jung's. Jung relates this universal connecting principle to the alchemical Mercurius and so to the collective unconscious. Thus in his final conception of the unity worked by the spirit, Jung presents the picture of man unified in spirit, soul, and body, and through this inner unification connected with the principle of unity underlying all that which is. In presenting this picture Jung uses a term which is one of the central images in Tillich's thought, that of God as the "ground of being." Jung uses it to describe the final unity towards which the psyche moves, the same goal the alchemists sought with their "magic":

> The creation of unity by a magical procedure meant the possibility of effecting a union with the world—not with the world of multiplicity as we see it but with a potential world, the eternal Ground of all empirical being, just as the self is the ground and origin of the individual personality past, present, and future.[40]

This potential world contains all the possibilities that can come into actuality in the created world. It serves the same function in Jung's thought as does the essential in Tillich's. It points to that state of being from which all actuality has departed and towards which it tends as to its fullest realization. It refers to that aspect of the individual Jung calls the self, and Tillich calls essential manhood, which is distorted in existence and realized in never more than fragmentary form, though its very distortion points to a more whole, emerging personality. Jung too uses the term "essential" to describe "an incorruptible essence potentially present in every human being. ... the very ground of existence, the procreative urge, which is of fiery origin."[41] The point here is that Jung points to a power and process, that of the self, which moves man to a unified personality and a relationship with the ground of being, always close at hand as the basis of the psyche.

In his work on the Spirit (capital S, by which he means Holy Spirit), the fourth part of his system, Tillich begins with a general description of the nature of life. He defines life simply as the "actuality of being,"[42] a definition that includes even the inorganic. Everything represents a passage from essence to existence, and so is imbued with a drive back to its essential reality in the Godhead. As such everything is in some sense alive. Tillich relates this extended sense of life both to the categories of essence in existence striving back to its pristine expression, and to St. Paul's more poetic expression of the same truth, that all creation "groans" for its lost perfection.

Tillich goes on to deny the attribution of hierarchical levels to life. Rather he prefers to speak of "the multidimensional unity" of life.[43] For Tillich, talk of different levels implies discontinuities between nature and grace, or between the natural and supernatural. Tillich rejects this conception in favour of one more akin to Nicholas of Cusa's conception of the coincidence of opposites. Tillich's position is that the conception of the multidimensional unity of life is capable of showing how all the dimensions of life inhere in one centre. In man this centre unifies in itself the three dimensions which in Tillich's view constitute the human, namely the biological, psychological, and spiritual. All dimensions meet in the same point. Again, in human life this centre is spiritual and so free, capable of knowledge and moral response.

What Tillich is trying to avoid here is any form of determinism or reductionism, biological or psychological, which would deny the freedom of the Spirit, as well as any form of dualism which would split the Spirit from its inherence in and conditioning by the psychological and biological. Thus Tillich has a tripartite understanding of the levels of life comparable to Jung's understanding of body, soul, and spirit. Like Jung, Tillich understands the process of healthy growth to be one in which these dimensions of life come into closer unity. For in the conditions of existence, under the power of the biological or psychological, man could fail to attain his spiritual freedom, or having attained it lose it to the lesser dimensions of his humanity.

For Tillich, therefore, the personal centre is threatened in existence not by the fact that it unites in itself the biological, psychological, and spiritual, as though they were in themselves inimical or hostile one to the other. Rather the threat lies in the fact that the spiritual might fail to come into a position of predominance and so harmoniously integrate the other dimensions. In this sense Spirit works to bring about, and is itself, the product of the unity of the multidimensional wealth that should coalesce in the personal centre of life.

The Spirit also works to unify what Tillich calls the ontological polarities. Tillich conceives of these opposites in tension as very significant aspects of life. They are polarities which, in a successful life process, must be brought into a unity which preserves their separateness even as it unites them. In this Tillich echoes Jung's understanding of energy as deriving from opposition. Unless these opposites are brought into a unity which yet preserves their tension, then one may consume the other, or they might fall into unrelatedness, pulling life into their split. Again Tillich's thought here parallels Jung's emphasis on one-sidedness as a major symptom of neurosis.

For Tillich the overriding polarity is that between self and other. Under this general polarity Tillich distinguishes three more in his work on Spirit, giving them a prominence greater than already seen in his thought on God as the union of opposites. The three polarities are self-identity and self-alteration, potentiality and its actualization, and freedom and destiny.

Tillich relates the first polarity to the process of remaining oneself while going out to others. This involves relationality, especially at the intrapersonal level. Tillich describes it as the process of self-integration, the very substance of morality. The union of opposites in this area of life results in centredness. Failure results in the disintegration of life, in disease. Ideally, Tillich depicts this aspect of life as circular: life flows to the other and back to oneself, enriching both.

The second polarity is really that between power and form or meaning. It is of more importance to Tillich than the other two because he defines Spirit as the unity of power and meaning, and attributes to God as Spirit the all-encompassing meaning of the Godhead. Thus Spirit for Tillich implies the reality of God as Trinity. It also implies, since all life participates in the Trinity and is destined to intensify this participation, that the polarity of power and meaning is one in which human life most images in its own flow the flow of divine life. This polarity is for Tillich at the basis of self-creation. It is the substance of culture, and works towards the new in personal and cultural life. Successful integration in this area produces growth. Unsuccessful integration of these polarities results in death. In this sphere the human spirit must grow or die. Tillich visualizes this movement of the Spirit as horizontal, from centre to ever more inclusive centre.

The third polarity, that between freedom and destiny, Tillich relates to self-transcendence and so to the specifically religious dimension of life. Integration of these opposites introduces the sublime into life as life moves vertically to its destined unity with God. Failure in this aspect of life results in profanization, a loss of the sense of one's personal holiness and so of the holiness of all life.

Tillich's general position is that Spirit functions to unite the opposites in each of the major polarities of life. Thus it works towards self-integration or morality, towards self-creation or culture, and towards self-transcendence or religion. But Tillich sees an even greater effect of the Spirit, in terms of unifying these three major aspects of life themselves. In such an ultimate unity of morality, culture, and religion, the reality of each would be preserved but not in conflictual tension. The power of God would flow through all, but in a manner that respects the intrinsic demands of each.

This vision of so intense a unity of all the dimensions of life remains for Tillich precisely that, a vision of a final eschatological unity of man's spirit with the Holy Spirit. Yet it is that towards which the Spirit historically moves, leading man and creation back from existence to their essential character as fully grounded in and transparent to the divine. In this transparency all opposites and tensions relate nondestructively in the final unity of man with all aspects of himself and his life.

However, the inevitable distortions of essence in existence mean that the opposites tend to separate and destroy life. We have described how this may happen in a personal life. Similar destructive tensions can occur among the three major expressions of the human spirit. For instance, morality that is attached to a commitment to a religion can be hostile to the moral values that may be expressed in a culture from a secular or humanistic basis, just as such moralities may reject religious moralities as constrictive impositions. Similarly, culture can turn against religion itself in an attitude which Tillich calls self-sufficient finitude. Or religion can declare itself in possession of an absolute truth and war against the autonomy of morality and culture.

In these wider domains of life, as in the personal, the Spirit works to unite the hostile opposites. In fact it is true to say that in Tillich's thought whatever is held together, personally or socially, is done so by the Spirit. Thus whatever fragmentary unities may exist among morality, culture, and religion are the work of the Spirit. Tillich occasionally points to the High Middle Ages as an historical instance when these unities were more highly realized in a theonomous society. By this Tillich is not glorifying the Middle Ages as an ideal to which a return is possible, nor as an age intrinsically holier than others. He simply points to it as to a time when religion, art, and morality interpenetrated organically, transfused by a common bond yet each respecting the autonomy of the others.

In a sense Tillich implies that the Spirit functions to oppose disintegration and to support integration. Yet he does want to establish a framework in which the Spirit is discernibly and dramatically present as a power which grasps man, and leads him into unambiguous or essential life no matter how fragmentary it be. Here Tillich again uses his essential-existential dialectic, showing that in terms of life's continuous participation in essence, the Spirit is present always. "Since the Spirit means 'God present,'" he writes, "no human form of life and thought can be shut off from the Spirit."[44] Yet beyond this residual presence, in moments of impressive religious experience or inspiration, the Spirit grasps and leads man into experiences of an unqualified, unambiguous life. Man cannot confer these on himself; they are in fact the object of his deepest longing and at the same time the ultimate meaning of his life.

Thus Tillich speaks of a mutual immanence of the divine and the human: "In the human spirit's essential relation to the divine Spirit, there is no correlation, but rather, mutual immanence."[45] In existence this essential relation is not and cannot be activated by man. Its activation is always a divine initiative. This situation, for Tillich, "illustrates the truth that the human spirit is unable to compel the divine Spirit to enter the human spirit."[46] But though the Spirit comes to man only on its own terms and at its own initiative, yet it is also constantly present to the human condition as the basis of man's thirst for it. Tillich describes this dialectic when he writes, "If God were not also in man so that man could ask for God, God's speaking to man could not be perceived by man."[47]

On these points Tillich and Jung are in broad agreement. Theologian and psychologist concur that the experience of the Spirit both grips consciousness as if from beyond and is a force which the ego cannot manipulate. In this Tillich and Jung are addressing the perennial problem of man's cooperation with the Spirit or with grace. Tillich holds such cooperation to be both necessary and legitimate. Indeed, his theological anthropology depicts man as constantly aware of the presence of God in his depths. This is the basis of Tillich's conception of man as ultimately concerned. Thus Jung could be hasty in describing as necessarily heretical the alchemist's efforts to elicit an immediate experience of the Spirit, especially since the alchemist may have been aware that the experience he sought was of a power greater than that of his ego.

Jung and Tillich also share similar conclusions on the effects of the Spirit. Tillich's criteria for the discernment of the Spirit in man easily correlate with psychological growth. In order of importance he lists increasing awareness, increasing freedom, increasing relatedness, and an increasing sense of transcendence.[48]

The first criterion relates directly to depth psychology, and to the process of becoming aware of the forces, both divine and demonic, which are operative in and around any life process. Such deepened awareness becomes then the occasion for "affirming life and its vital dynamics in spite of its ambiguities."[49] Tillich also understands depth psychology as contributing to the second criterion of the presence of Spirit to life, namely that of increasing freedom. Thus he sees the Spirit acting through depth psychology "to liberate men from particular compulsions which are impediments to growth in Spiritual freedom."[50]

Again, in terms of increased relatedness, Tillich points to the contributions the psychotherapeutic world has made in calling the individual back from "self-seclusion."[51] He believes, just as Jung does, that only the internal relatedness to one's own depths or heights enables relationship to an actual other. In other words, as one attains one's essential self, which is grounded in God, one automatically relates to the whole, because the essential self is expressed in the Logos as the source of all that can be. To the extent that the individual achieves this, essential self-identity and relatedness become one. This unity with one's essential self in the ground of being is experienced as the holy or self-transcendence, the fourth criterion of Spirit.

In these passages the term "essential self,"[52] in function and meaning, is closely akin to Jung's conception of the self. And just as Jung doubts that this self is ever fully achieved in existence but only approximated, so Tillich believes that the perfect, unambiguous life symbolized by the essential self is never more than fragmentarily realized:

> The Christian life never reaches the state of perfection—it always remains an up-and-down course—but in spite of its mutable character it contains a movement toward maturity, however fragmentary the mature state may be.[53]

Tillich and Jung also have similar views regarding the far reaching unities the Spirit can work. Tillich understands the Spirit to elevate man into "the transcendent unity of the divine life and in so doing it reunites the estranged existence of the person with his essence."[54] This process works personally to establish the individual in his self-integration, self-creation, and self-transcendence. Collectively it leads to unities of morality, culture, and religion. The process is based upon the Spirit bringing the "personal centre" of the individual life into unity with "the universal centre." It is the same process Jung describes in terms of the unity of the microcosm with the macrocosm, which he identifies as the substance of both the *anthropos* symbol and the *unus mundus*, the ultimate healing unity.

6 Church, Morality, and Eschatology

Discussion of spirit and the Holy Spirit moves naturally to a consideration of the Church as the community of Spirit, morality as life lived in the Spirit, and the eschaton as the culmination towards which personal and collective life move when guided by the Spirit.

For both Tillich and Jung, the reality of the Church cannot be reduced to any particular visible body. For Tillich the Church is the Spiritual Community, potentially universal and actualized wherever the New Being or essential humanity is being worked. This community can be found both within and beyond formal ecclesial groups.

In Jung's view, the Spirit manifests in any and every life in which movement towards the self is taking place. This position does not prevent him from paying frequent tribute to the Christian symbols as possessing the power, when properly appreciated, to foster the process of individuation. Indeed, he feels that in the West, "a real and essentially religious renewal can be based...only on Christianity."[1] He believes that imported religions are ultimately inadequate to the spiritual needs of Western man because we lack the corresponding historical roots.[2]

As already seen, however, Jung's appreciation of Christianity is not at all unqualified. Besides Christianity's difficulties with the problems of evil, matter, and the feminine, it has lost, in Jung's opinion—and here he is certainly joined by Tillich—an appreciation of the symbolic. The consequent literalism has turned the mind of the believer to an external God and to an historical Christ, away from the internal realities of both. Jung calls for an internalization of the import and impact of the Christian symbols, in order to acquaint the believer with that level of his psyche which originally produced these symbols, and still does. Thus, for instance, Jung argues that the symbol of the *anthropos* is the substance of the Christian myth and yet is older in its Egyptian, Persian, and Hellenic background than Christianity itself.[3] For Jung, to come into the Spirit is to come under the guiding influence of those internal powers operating on behalf of the self which lead man to his interior unity and to a sense of his unity with the whole.

Regarding the split within Christianity, Jung and Tillich show an appreciation and a critical valuation of both major traditions. Tillich talks frequently of Catholic substance and Protestant principle, believing that the Catholic, sacramental, and priestly position must be present in tension with the Protestant, prophetic, and critical tradition if Christianity is to be whole. Tillich's conception of sacramentalism ultimately rests on his view that all of being participates in the ground of being, and so being is potentially transparent to the divine in such a way that the divine can appear through it, though never be unqualifiedly identified with that through which it appears.

For Tillich all of reality, including the mind, is potentially sacramental. As the mind moves into its own depths it becomes the vehicle through which the divine appears in the form of symbols, whose content is taken from the external event. Because of this innate susceptibility of the mind to be approached from its own depths with the sense of the divine, Tillich is very appreciative of the "discovery" of the unconscious by modern psychology. He associates the origins of man's experience of the Spirit with the unconscious and so, like Jung, sees the unconscious operative in that experience.[4]

In the same vein Tillich writes that if man is seen as only intellectual, then only "words" can touch him, and, in this truncated view of man, "No Spirit-bearing objects or acts, nothing sensuous which affects the unconscious, can be accepted."[5] In a further tribute to depth psychology Tillich adds that "the twentieth-century re-discovery of the unconscious" has contributed to a positive reevaluation of "the sacramental mediation of the Spirit."[6] In this context he also reaffirms that the Spirit grasps man in his totality and, since this totality includes the unconscious, the Spirit must also touch man at this level of his being. But a theology of the Word can touch only the rational part of man. "One could even say," writes Tillich, "that a Spiritual Presence apprehended through consciousness alone is intellectual and not truly Spiritual."[7] Thus Tillich defends an understanding of the sacramental principle as pointing to the divine depths of the human psyche. Any theology or derivative spirituality that cannot address the unconscious cannot, therefore, address the total man and thus tends to confine rather than to heal. In fact Tillich is so aware of the depths in nature calling to the depths in man, in sacramental interplay, that he attributes a peculiar power to certain material realities to mediate an experience of the Spirit to man. He writes, "The Spirit 'uses' the powers of being in nature in order to 'enter' man's spirit."[8]

In tension with this radical sacramentalism Tillich posits the Protestant principle. This is a critical principle which states that though the reality of God can appear through any segment of created reality —because all of reality is grounded in God—no created reality through which the divine appears can be identified with God. This identification would be formal idolatry. Tillich applies this principle to his understanding of ecclesial authority, to demonic sacramentalism, and even to Christ himself. To the extent that Catholicism, for instance, identifies itself or its authority with the divine and so absolutizes itself, it falls victim to the Protestant principle. The error consists in "the identification of an organized church with the presence of the Divine in history, and the consequent claim for absoluteness by this church."[9]

In accord with this critical principle Tillich further argues that sacraments as individual acts can be demonized if, as the reformers claim, they were given a quasi-automatic efficacy through the Catholic doctrine of *opus operatum*. This doctrine could be read to mean that the efficacy of the sacraments was attributed to "mere performance" which easily degenerates into "a magical technique."[10] Tillich gives to this very traditional argument against Catholic sacramental magic a peculiarly modern interpretation. He argues that such magical use of the sacraments touches or manipulates the unconscious without the participation of consciousness. He sees this as a subtle coercion of the "centred self." To Tillich, being aware of these different possibilities is of crucial importance. If the unconscious is affected without conscious participation, the personality is being manipulated and violated. On the other hand, if one is conscious of the depths at which one is moved by sacramental power, one then fully and humanly participates in the sacramental act, allowing it to enter and to transform.[11]

Even in his Christology, Tillich's Protestant principle is at work. As already shown, Tillich understands the significance of Christ to be the realization of essential humanity in existence. Through the symbols which grow out of this event this essential humanity is mediated to others. However, Tillich feels that to focus on the details of the historical life of Jesus, and not to see the meaning of his life as the bearer of man's essence and New Being, is to miss the point of the event and to become idolatrously fixed on the peripheral through which the essential appeared. Thus in Tillich's view, a major meaning of the crucifixion is the destruction of Jesus' individual and personal traits so that his universal meaning might emerge.

Jung too shows a warm appreciation of the sacramental principle, especially in the form of ritual reenactment and symbolic expression.[12] He speaks favourably of Catholic sacramentalism, symbolism, and ritual as realities that have proceeded from the unconscious, and which retain a strong capacity to lead man back into it if their power is sensitively appreciated and responded to. He sees them as providing "a worthy receptacle for the plethora of figures in the unconscious."[13] However, like Tillich, Jung is cautious about the way the sacraments are surrounded by the absolute authority of the Church.

This authoritarianism he views dimly and with a certain regret.

Jung's evaluation and criticism of Protestantism is equally nuanced. Protestantism, he argues, broke the contained access to the unconscious provided by the sacraments.[14] He points out, for instance, that the German vitalities that broke the sacramental mediation have since been with difficulty contained, and have taken on rather dubious expressions.[15] Thus the consequences of the Reformation for Jung are both positive and negative. Positively, it offered to the individual the possibility of direct, immediate access to the fiery experience of the divine.[16] Negatively, it meant that few people could achieve or sustain this immediacy in the intensity of its demands. Furthermore, the individual was called upon to face the reality of guilt without benefit of sacramental relief.[17] Jung feels that this could purify and "sharpen" one's conscience.[18] The Reformation tended to foster conscious individuality, but this finally worked to break Protestant Christianity into many divisions, a development Jung frequently laments. This same emphasis on consciousness led to a literalism which gradually became insensitive to symbolic understanding, especially of the New Testament itself.[19] Jung thinks very little of efforts at demythologizing, if by the term is meant the effort to divest the New Testament of its mythical power.

Thus Tillich and Jung both appreciate and criticize the two major camps of Christianity in similar ways. They express a profound appreciation of the sacramental principle, because it is so closely associated with the very possibility of religion itself and in that sense precedes the criticism of religion as the sacramental precedes the iconoclastic, though it ever stands in need of it. Both closely relate the reality of the sacramental to the reality of the unconscious. They are equally aware of the demonic possibilities of sacramentalism. When it takes the form of the reduction of the means of grace to that of ecclesial mediation, it can become an aspect of a power drive. When the sacraments are identified with the ultimate, rather than seen as aspects of reality through which the ultimate can appear, they are formally idolatrous. When the sacramental is so used that it touches the unconscious without the engagement of the ego, it can be profoundly manipulative. Against these possibilities both Tillich and Jung affirm the need for conscious criticism and distance. For Tillich this is the function of the Protestant principle. For Jung it means retaining ego even as the ego incarnates its unconscious depths. For both, then, the critical principle functions to prevent the ego being overwhelmed or manipulated by the unconscious.

In a manner which could be of considerable value for ecumenical discussion, Tillich and Jung proffer a critical validation of the principles on which Catholicism and Protestantism rest. The Catholic principle, that of sacramentality, is more intimately related to the unconscious but can lead to idolatry or the manipulation of consciousness. The Protestant principle strongly affirms consciousness, but can lead into a superficiality which ultimately severs the ego from the unconscious. With this severance comes the accompanying insensitivity to symbol, the language of religion and of the unconscious.

Historically, the differentiation between these principles is roughly analogous to the differentiation between the ego and the unconscious. In Western Christianity the time of conjunction could be at hand, providing each side would recognize its complementary need of the other. Both Jung and Tillich strongly believe that living in either principle exclusively cannot provide a wholesome spiritual life. Thus Jung writes, perhaps with a touch of irony, that after the Reformation alchemy for the Protestant was the only way of being a Catholic.[20] By this he means that Protestantism removed its adherents from the immediate religious experience of the unconscious, which remained available to the Catholic through sacramentalism. However, Jung also points out that even Catholic Christians had recourse to the alchemical immediacy of experience which, apparently, was lacking to their lives even with access to the sacraments.

For his part, Tillich sought to reintroduce into modern Protestantism something of the mysticism that had been lost since the demise of nineteenth-century romantic theology (which reached its heights with Schleiermacher). As a theologian he attempts such a synthesis in his massive *Systematic Theology,* where the complementarity of Catholic substance and Protestant principle is shown to be of major importance to a wholesome and mature Christian spirituality. Jung, also intensely aware of the split, sought first and foremost to bring together these opposing principles in his own psyche. In his letters he writes that such efforts to unite the opposites in himself were not always well received: "The fact that I as a Christian struggle to unite Catholicism and Protestantism within myself is chalked up against me in true Pharisaic fashion as blatant proof of lack of character."[21] To unite opposites that have become hardened in collective religious conflict is not easy. Yet the effort to bring them together was a central concern, task, and source of suffering for both Jung and Tillich.

The moral imperative that emerges in their work is again based on the fidelity of the individual to his true self. For Tillich this is the essential self, which he grounds theologically in God and towards

which each life moves by its inner dynamic. He calls this a theonomous morality, because it is based on the demand in the life of every
individual to submit to the law of God's presence as the law of one's
essential humanity. The process of approaching or assimilating one's
essential self is for Tillich the work of the Holy Spirit. It is experienced as grace because it unites man with God. As such it is also
experienced as both love and suffering or sacrifice, because it comes
from a source beyond one's conscious control, often as a consequence of personal loss or disintegration. Tillich describes the
experience as "the reality of that which the law commands, the
reunion with one's true being, and this means the reunion with
oneself, with others, and with the ground of one's self and others."[22]

And yet the fulfillment of the moral imperative, which is in effect
the gift of self, is also experienced as sacrifice because all that stands
in the way of the essential self must be removed. In this sense the
sacrifice Tillich proposes is analogous to the suffering described by
Jung in the process of individuation, particularly as it applies to the
sacrifice of ego consciousness to the "priesthood" of the unconscious
(as detailed in his work on the Mass). Tillich writes of this process of
suffering towards the self in these terms:

> In the 'communion of the Holy Spirit,' the essential being of the
> person is liberated from the contingencies of freedom and destiny
> under the conditions of existence. The acceptance of this liberation is
> the all-inclusive sacrifice which, at the same time, is the all-inclusive
> fulfilment.[23]

For Tillich, then, the law of morality is the law of one's essential
being. It can be fulfilled only through the initiative of the Spirit.
This experience is always qualified by love and by the pain of being
led into one's essential being. The basis of one's response to life is
then the love that becomes conscious as the individual becomes
conscious of his true self. Tillich writes that "with respect to moral
content, theonomous morality is determined by Spirit-created
love."[24] This means that the ultimate determinants of moral choices
are not universal laws that might be derived from reason, as in
philosophical ethics. Nor is the ultimate authority a revealed morality imposed on man from beyond (though Tillich recommends that
traditional morality be taken seriously, since it usually represents
some collective wisdom). Rather the ultimate factor is love, which
attaches to the process of man's becoming essential and which is
applied to each individual act in all its particulars. Tillich writes that
"[morality] is made concrete and adequate by the application of the
courage of love to the unique situation."[25] Such "courage of love" is
the work of the Spirit.

Though Jung seldom uses such terms as "grace" to describe the process of coming into greater approximation of the self, yet he does describe this process in terms of the interaction of the ego with powers greater than itself. The nature of Jung's conception of morality is best brought out in his conflict with Freud, where Jung bluntly denies that the ultimate demand on man derives from "collective moral consciousness" or from the introjection of collective values, demands, and inhibitions. He considers Freud's view that conscience is formed entirely through the internalization of parental or societal restraints as inadequate to human dignity and to the demands of the higher self.[26] Rather for Jung the ultimate moral demand comes from the self, in the interests of "the more compendious personality," a demand that is at once personal and interior. Concerning the sacrifice required on behalf of the self, Jung writes:

> I renounce my claim because I feel impelled to do so for painful inner reasons which are not altogether clear to me. These reasons give me no particular moral satisfaction; on the contrary, I even feel some resistance to them. But I must yield to the power which surpasses my egoistic claim. Here the self is integrated; it is withdrawn from projection and has become perceptible as a determining psychic factor.[27]

In these words Jung takes a position not unlike Tillich's. The ultimate moral determinant engrained in the fabric of the individual is to become oneself. With Tillich this is the work of the Spirit. With Jung the achievement of the self is not only a holy experience but *the* experience of the holy. Speaking of the union of the unconscious and the ego worked in and by the self, Jung writes, "The self then functions as a union of opposites and thus constitutes the most immediate experience of the Divine which it is psychologically possible to imagine."[28]

*

Tillich, the systematic theologian, as might be expected has a highly developed eschatology. Since he locates the essential both in man and in eternity, he takes the position that the end of the temporal processes and of human life is always eternally present. "The eternal," he writes, "is not a future state of things. It is always present, not only in man (who is aware of it), but also in everything that has being within the whole of being."[29] Thus the move towards the final end of life, which Tillich terms "eternal blessedness," consists of a process of "essentialization."[30] This process is one wherein each life, having left its purely potential state of "dreaming innocence" and entered into existence, works towards a reunion with its essence. In other words, each life opting for or against its essence creates itself, or is created by the Spirit in time and existence, and in so doing contributes "to the Kingdom of God in its fulfilment."[31] Judgement consists of a process in which the degree of essentialization achieved in a lifetime is revealed to the individual by death, which strips away the nonessential. Of the revelation of the essential through death, Tillich writes:

> Participation in the eternal life depends on a creative synthesis of a being's essential nature with what it has made of it in its temporal existence. In so far as the negative has maintained possession of it, it is exposed in its negativity and excluded from eternal memory. Whereas, in so far as the essential has conquered existential distortion its standing is higher in eternal life.[32]

This position is the logical conclusion of Tillich's doctrine of the Spirit as it works in life, elevating the personal centre into the centredness of divine life, and so ultimately into eternity and what Tillich calls blessedness. Tillich's point, already made in his thought on the Trinity as reciprocal flow between abyss and form, is that the divine life itself is blessed because the note of negativity in it is constantly overcome. "It is the nature of blessedness itself," he writes, "that requires a negative element in the eternity of the Divine Life."[33] Divine life is thus "the eternal conquest of the negative."[34]

The process of essentialization, then, is one in which a human life, having been led into its essential self fragmentarily in time and in existence, participates eternally, to whatever degree this participation has been realized in time, in the balance and vitality of divine life, in which the negative is eternally overcome. Beyond this Tillich refuses to say more, deferring to the speculation of religious poets.

Tillich does believe, however, that the processes of essentialization are in some sense truly universal. For instance, he denies the doctrine that the final state can be one of an ultimate separation of the saved and the damned. For Tillich this view has "demonic implications," for "it introduces an eternal split into God himself."[35] The reason is that the essential is grounded in both God and man. Were humanity to be eternally divided into the accepted and the rejected, God himself would be involved in this eternal bifurcation and would remain frustrated in bringing to a unified outcome what he had initiated as creator.

Thus Tillich's thought leads by its inner dynamic to some form of a universal recapitulation, an *apocastastasis*. Ultimately, he believes that the life of the individual and individual freedom is bound up with the destiny of the whole of humanity. As grounded in God, each essential self participates in the other, and all participate in the destiny of regaining a common ground and origin:

> Freedom and destiny in every individual are united in such a way that it is as impossible to separate one from the other as it is, consequently, to separate the eternal destiny of any individual from the destiny of the whole race and of being in all its manifestations.[36]

In thise sense the humanity of the most distorted life participates in that of the greatest; e.g., the sinner is in the saint (and vice versa). Tillich writes that "in the essence of the least actualized individual, the essences of other individuals and, indirectly, of all beings are present."[37]

Tillich's eschatology is therefore closely related to a profound hope. He strikes the dual notes of the importance of man's response to the lure, challenge, and demand of becoming essential—always aware of the possibility of self-loss—coupled with the triumphant note that the essential as grounded in God can never be lost. Hence he denies the literal truth of the opposites of "eternal death" and "the security of the return."[38] The former rules out the rendering eternal of the split in humanity and so in divinity into two ultimate and opposed segments. The latter forbids an inhuman presumption which would take lightly the use of man's freedom in the recovery of his essence. Something can be lost. But in this dialectic, where truth lies in neither of the poles alone, Tillich yet seems to favour "the security of the return," because man's being is grounded in God and as such the gates of hell or nonbeing cannot prevail against it.

Jung's eschatology is not so systematically elaborated. But he would agree with Tillich's vision of a final essentialization, in that the experience of God, the eternal, and the unity of all things is possible due to man's archetypal constitution, and manifests in those images of wholeness which have traditionally been associated with images of God.

In this respect Jung's conception of the *anthropos* is related to Tillich's notion of essentialization, wherein the individual experiences his community with God. Both agree that the goal of life is this final unity. Tillich, though he realizes it is a reality which can only be expressed symbolically, and that rational analysis of the symbol can threaten its power or native impact, does seem to see this final unity as destined and one in which every individual will participate. Jung's eschatology is rather more reserved, in that it focuses on the personal moral dimension, that is, on one's personal movement towards the self in the context of the present.

One of the better expressions of Jung's thought on the eschaton is contained in a letter he wrote to Father Victor White in 1953.[39] Here

Jung emphasizes that the meaning of the Christ symbol is still very relevant, for it focuses on the opposition between good and evil.[40] He repeats his belief that modern society "has not even begun to face its shadow," and contends that only out of this conflict fully undergone can the dawning of the age of the Spirit come.[41] Only then is the symbol of Christ to be transcended in the age of the Spirit:

> It is true however that the *imitatio Christi* leads you into your own very real and *Christlike conflict* with darkness, and the more you are engaged in this war and in these attempts at peacemaking helped by the anima, the more you begin to look forward beyond the Christian aeon to the *Oneness of the Holy Spirit*. He is the *pneumatic state the creator attains to through the phase of incarnation*. He is the experience of every individual that has undergone the complete abolition of his ego through the absolute opposition expressed by the symbol Christ versus Satan.[42]

Then Jung points to what the substance of the age of the Spirit would be:

> The state of the Holy Spirit means a restitution of the original oneness of the unconscious on the level of consciousness. That is alluded to, as I see it, by Christ's logion: 'Ye are gods.' This state is not quite understandable yet. It is a mere anticipation.[43]

The state of the Holy Spirit here described by Jung, analogous to Tillich's description of essentialization, involves the unambiguous unity of the ego with the unconscious at the conscious level. If God is mediated through the unconscious, this condition would be one in which the ego is fully pervaded with the sense of God. It is a psychological explanation of what is described in apocalyptic literature as the realization that God is "all in all." While Jung sees this as the direction in which personal and universal psyche moves, a state in which opposites such as Christ and devil, good and evil, are transcended, he does believe that the recognition and conscious assimilation of the shadow is the task of the modern age. For this task, writes Jung, "Christ is still the valid symbol."[44]

Also in this revealing letter, Jung advises Father White to stay in the Church and to make known to the times the full import of the symbol of Christ and the meaning of the conflict with Satan. Jung obviously felt that White shared something of his vision of the coming of a new age of consciousness, an age of the Spirit, for he points out that some "must stay behind their vision in order to help and to teach."[45] Thus the constellation of the opposites, and the implied challenge to bring about their unity on a higher spiritual plane, is for Jung close to the substance of the contribution Christianity has made to the human spirit and to this aion. Only if this challenge is met can the Christian age be transcended. Indeed, Jung is of the opinion that such transcendence is itself the work of God.

Tillich's eschatology contains the demand that man look within to his essential self, to discover there the "courage to be." Jung's eschatology demands an ongoing battle with the shadow, the internalization of the conflict between the opposites, in the expectation that the attendant suffering will give birth to the transcendent function or self. Each in his own way affirms that man will come into the eschaton only if he takes full responsibility for his personal psychic or spiritual state. Responsibility, for both Tillich and Jung, means the conscious confrontation of the powers, demonic and divine, which man meets in his own psyche. Thus the realization of the age of the Spirit depends to no small extent on man's moral response to himself and the powers that rage within. And in this vital work performed in the depths of the human soul, the psychological task and the religious task are one.

Notes

CW—Collected Works of C.G. Jung (Bollingen Series XX). 20 vols. Transl. R.F.C. Hull. Princeton: Princeton University Press, 1953-1979.

DF—Paul Tillich, *Dynamics of Faith.* New York: Harper & Row, 1956.

Letters I, II—C.G. Jung, *Letters* (Bollingen Series XCV). 2 vols. Transl. R.F.C. Hull. Princeton: Princeton University Press, 1973.

MDR—C.G. Jung, *Memories, Dreams, Reflections.* Transl. Richard and Clara Winston. New York: Random House, Vintage Books, 1961.

ST I, II, II—Paul Tillich, *Systematic Theology.* 3 vols. Chicago: University of Chicago Press, 1956-1964.

TC—Paul Tillich, *Theology of Culture.* New York: Oxford University Press, 1959.

1   The Apologetic Problem

1. See *MDR*, pp. x-xi, where Aniela Jaffe writes: "From the viewpoint of dogmatic Christianity, Jung was distinctly an 'outsider.' ... More than once he said grimly, 'They would have burned me as a heretic in the Middle Ages!'"

2. *ST* I, p. 139.

3. "Psychology and Religion," *Psychology and Religion, CW* 11, pars. 16, 18.

4. *MDR*, pp. 42-43: "When I heard him preaching about grace, I always thought of my own experience. What he said sounded stale and hollow, like a tale told by someone who knows it only by hearsay and cannot quite believe it himself."

5. Ibid., p. 92.

6. "Background to the Psychology of Christian Alchemical Symbolism," *Aion, CW* 9ii, par. 276.

7. *ST* I, p. 90.

8. *Perspectives on 19th and 20th Century Protestant Theology* (New York: Harper & Row, 1967) pp. 75, 94. Here Tillich refers to the inhesion of the finite and the infinite in terms of a mutual "within-each-otherness."

9. *MDR*, p. 45.

10. Ibid., pp. 52-53.

11. "A Psychological Approach to the Dogma of the Trinity," *CW* 11.

12. *MDR*, p. 62.

13. Ibid.

14. "Psychology and Religion," *CW* 11, par. 4: "The idea is psychologically true inasmuch as it exists. Psychological existence is subjective in so far as an idea occurs in only one individual. But it is objective in so far as that idea is shared by a society—by a *consensus gentium.*"

15. "The Problem of Types in the History of Classical and Medieval Thought,"*Psychological Types, CW* 6, pars. 59-67.

16. *MDR*, p. 55.

17. Ibid., p. 93.

18. Ibid., p. 94.

19. Ibid., p. 95.

20. "Psychotherapists or the Clergy," *CW* 11, par. 509: "Among all my patients in the second half of life—that is to say, over thirty-five—there has not been one whose problem in the last resort was not that of finding a religious outlook on life.... This of course has nothing to do with a particular creed or membership of a church."

21. *DF*, p. 16.

22. Ibid., p. 12.

23. "The Problem of Types," *CW* 6, par. 67.

24. "Two Types of Philosophy of Religion," *TC*, pp. 10-29.

25. Ibid., p. 17.

26. *DF*, p. 4.

27. Ibid.

28. Ibid., pp. 4-5.

29. Ibid., Chapter 2, "What Faith is Not."

30. Ibid., p. 6.

31. Ibid.

32. "Transformation Symbolism in the Mass," *CW* 11, par. 390.

33. *DF*, p. 9.

34. "A Psychological Approach to the Trinity," *CW* 11, par. 295.

35. *TC*, p. 13.

36. *ST* I, p. 6.

37. Ibid., p. 62.

38. *Letters* 1, p. 471: "It would indeed be a great surprise to me if anything at all should come out of dialectical theology that might be of practical interest to human beings.... it has always remained dark to me exactly what the dialogue is supposed to consist of. To me it seems completely absent." See also p. 331, where Jung refers to "that grizzler Kierkegaard" as a psychopath, and *Letters* II, p. 145: "Regarding your detailed account of Kierkegaard, I was once again struck by the discrepancy between the perpetual talk about fulfilling God's will and reality: when God appeared to him in the shape of 'Regina' he took to his heels."

39. *ST* I, p. 64.

40. Ibid., p. 65.

41. Ibid.

42. Ibid., pp. 6-8.

43. Ibid., p. 7.

44. *Letters* II, p. 115.

45. "Psychology and Religion," *CW* 11, par. 102.

46. "A Psychological Approach to the Trinity," *CW* 11.

47. *ST* III, p. 285.

48. *ST* I, pp. 216, 250-251.

49. *DF*, p. 11.

50. *ST* I, p. 61.

51. *The Interpretation of History* (New York: Scribner's, 1936), pp. 84ff.

52. "Answer to Job," *CW* 11.

53. *ST* I, p. 7.

54. *Letters* II, p. 67.

55. *ST* II, p. 16.

56. "Psychology and Religion," *CW* 11, par. 4.

57. "Archetypes of the Collective Unconscious," *The Archetypes and the Collective Unconscious, CW* 9i, par. 49.

58. "The Theological Significance of Existentialism and Psychoanalysis," *TC,* p. 123.

59. Ibid.

60. *ST* III, p. 207.

61. Ibid., p. 211.

62. "Existentialism and Psychoanalysis," *TC,* p. 124.

63. *ST* III, p. 243.

64. *A Memorial Meeting* (New York: Analytical Psychology Club, 1962), p. 31.

65. "Existentialism and Psychoanalysis," *TC,* p. 122.

66. *A Memorial Meeting,* p. 32.

67. *ST* I, pp. 130-131: "There is no revealed psychology just as there is no revealed historiography or revealed physics. It is not the task of theology to protect the truth of revelation by attacking Freudian doctrines of libido, repression, and sublimation on religious grounds or by defending a Jungian doctrine of man in the name of revelatory knowledge."

68. "Existentialism and Psychoanalysis," *TC,* p. 122.

69. Ibid.

70. Ibid., p. 120.

71. "The Depth of Reason," *ST* I, pp. 79-81.

72. Ibid., p. 136.

73. Ibid., pp. 158, 237-238.

74. Ibid., p. 134: "The pantheistic element in the classical doctrine that God is *ipsum esse,* being itself, is as necessary for a Christian doctrine of God as the mystical element of the divine presence." Cf. also *ST* II, p. 6, and *ST* III, p. 421, where Tillich refers to "eschatological pan-en-theism."

75. "Introduction to the Religious and Psychological Problems of Alchemy," *Psychology and Alchemy, CW* 12, pars. 10, 12. Here Jung deplores the fact that Western, Christian man places "all God outside."

76. "Dreaming Innocence and Temptation." *ST* II, pp. 33-36.

77. "The Visions of Zosimos," *Alchemical Studies, CW* 13, pars. 138-139.

78. *Letters* II, p. 502.

2 The Psyche as Sacrament

1. E.g. *Letters* I, p. 59, where Jung writes: "For me a symbol is the sensuously perceptible *expression of an inner experience.* A religious experience strives for expression and can be expressed only 'symbolically' because it transcends understanding. It *must* be expressed one way or another for therein is revealed its immanent vital force."

2. Tillich, *ST* III, p. 285.

3. *DF,* p. 45.

4. "Answer to Job," *Psychology and Religion, CW* 11, par. 647.

5. *Letters* II, p. 8: "I only fight *for* the reactivation of symbolic thinking, because of its therapeutic value, and *against* the presumptuous undervaluation of myth, which only a very few people have the least understanding of anyway."

6. *DF,* pp. 41-43.

7. Ibid., p. 43.

8. Ibid.

9. "The Problem of Types in the History of Classical and Medieval Thought," *Psychological Types, CW* 6, par. 93, n. 44. Cf. ibid., par. 788.

10. *Symbols of Transformation, CW* 5, par. 344.

11. *Letters* I, p. 62.

12. Ibid., p. 269.

13. "Concerning the Archetypes, with Special Reference to the Anima Concept," *The Archetypes and the Collective Unconscious, CW* 9i, par. 125.

14. *ST* I, pp. 132-135.

15. *Letters* I, p. 60.

16. Ibid., pp. 60-61.

17. *ST* I, p. 240.

18. Ibid.

19. Ibid., pp. 8-11.

20. Ibid., p. 73.

21. Ibid., p. 99.

22. "Psychotherapy or the Clergy," *CW* 11, par. 507.

23. *ST* I, p. 97.

24. Ibid., p. 238.

25. "The Depth of Reason," ibid., pp. 79-81.

26. Ibid., p. 80.

27. Ibid., p. 110.

28. Ibid., p. 116.

29. Ibid., p. 113.

30. Ibid., p. 11.

31. Ibid., p. 113.

32. Ibid.

33. Ibid., p. 117.

34. *ST* II, p. 97: "Christianity was born, not with the birth of the man who is called 'Jesus,' but in the moment in which one of his followers was driven to say to him, 'Thou art the Christ.'"

35. *CW* 5, par. 336.

36. Ibid.

37. *ST* I, p. 80.

38. *CW* 5, par. 335.

39. Ibid., par. 340.

40. Ibid.

41. Ibid.

42. Ibid., par. 341.
43. "A Psychological Approach to the Dogma of the Trinity," *CW* 11, par. 170.
44. *CW* 5, par. 345.
45. Ibid., par. 346.
46. Ibid., par. 30.
47. "Schiller's Ideas on the Type Problem," *CW* 6, par. 202.
48. Ibid.
49. "The Type Problem in Poetry," ibid., par. 424.
50. Ibid.
51. Ibid.
52. Ibid.
53. Ibid., par. 425.
54. Ibid.
55. Ibid.
56. Ibid.
57. Ibid., par. 427.
58. Ibid., par. 429.
59. Ibid., par. 427.
60. Ibid., par. 428.
61. Ibid., par. 432.
62. Ibid., par. 427.
63. "On Psychic Energy," *The Structure and Dynamics of the Psyche, CW* 8, par. 92.
64. Ibid.
65. Ibid., par. 110.
66. Ibid.
67. Ibid., par. 111.
68. Ibid.
69. "The Transcendent Function," *CW* 8, par. 145.
70. Ibid., par. 189.
71. Ibid., par. 193.
72. *The Courage to Be* (New Haven: Yale University Press, 1952).
73. "Definitions," *CW* 6, par. 819.
74. Ibid., par. 824.

3 God, the Union of Opposites, and the Trinity

1. *ST* I, p. 242.
2. Ibid., p. 250, and *ST* III, p. 285.
3. *ST* III, p. 283.
4. *ST* I, p. 221.
5. *ST* III, p. 283: "In the first consideration we have found that the more the ultimacy of the ultimate concern is emphasized, the more the religious need for a concrete manifestation of the divine develops, and the tension between the absolute and the concrete elements in the idea of God drives toward the establishment of divine figures between God and man."

6. *ST* II, p. 33.

7. Ibid., p. 44: "Creation is good in its essential character. If actualized, it falls into universal estrangement through freedom and destiny."

8. *ST* I, pp. 237-238.

9. Ibid., p. 250.

10. Ibid., p. 251: "The third principle is in a way the whole (God *is* Spirit), and in a way it is a special principle (God *has* the Spirit as he has the Logos)."

11. Ibid., pp. 174-186.

12. Ibid., pp. 245-249.

13. Ibid., pp. 234-235.

14. "A Psychological Approach to the Dogma of the Trinity," *Psychology and Religion, CW* 11, par. 171.

15. Ibid., par. 173.

16. Ibid., par. 178.

17. Ibid.

18. Ibid.

19. Ibid., par. 194.

20. Ibid., par. 204.

21. Ibid., par. 221.

22. Ibid.

23. Ibid., par. 233.

24. Ibid.

25. Ibid., par. 235.

26. Ibid., par. 273.

27. Ibid., par. 238.

28. Ibid., par. 239.

29. "The Problem of the Fourth," ibid., pars. 243-267.

30. *DF*, p. 11: "This is symbolically expressed by the mystics when they say that their knowledge of God is the knowledge God has of himself; and it is expressed by Paul when he says (1 Cor. 13) that he will know as he is known, namely, by God. God never can be object without being at the same time subject. Even a successful prayer, is, according to Paul (Rom. 8), not possible without God as Spirit praying within us."

31. *Mysterium Coniunctionis, CW* 14, par. 444.

32. Ibid., par. 760.

33. Ibid., par. 662.

34. *The Eternal Now* (New York: Charles Scribner's Sons, 1957).

35. "A Psychological Approach to the Trinity," *CW* 11, par. 289.

36. Ibid., par. 289.

37. "Psychology and Religion," ibid., par. 157.

38. "A Psychological Approach to the Trinity," ibid., par. 295.

4 The Search for the Nonhistorical Jesus

1. *Symbols of Transformation, CW* 5, par. 336.
2. *ST* II, pp. 98-113.
3. "Background to the Psychology of Christian Alchemical Symbolism," *Aion, CW* 9ii, par. 278.
4. Ibid.
5. *Letters* II, p. 75.
6. Ibid.
7. Ibid.
8. Ibid.: "How can you 'meet people in their lives' if you talk of things, and especially of unique events, that have *nothing* to do with human psyche?"
9. "Christian Alchemical Symbolism," *CW* 9ii, par. 283.
10. Ibid.
11. *Letters* II, p. 75.
12. "Christian Alchemical Symbolism," *CW* 9ii, par. 271.
13. Ibid.
14. Ibid.
15. "Christ, A Symbol of the Self," ibid., par. 69.
16. Ibid.
17. Ibid., par. 72.
18. Ibid.: "The scope of the integration is suggested by the *descensus ad inferos,* the descent of Christ's soul to hell, its work of redemption embracing even the dead."
19. Ibid.
20. Ibid., par. 73.
21. Ibid.
22. Ibid.
23. Ibid.
24. Ibid., par. 74.
25. Ibid., par. 122.
26. "Gnostic Symbols of the Self," ibid., par. 295.
27. *Letters* I, p. 66.
28. "The Historical Significance of the Fish," *CW* 9ii, par. 170.
29. "Archetypes of the Collective Unconscious," *The Archetypes and the Collective Unconscious, CW* 9i, par. 49.
30. "Significance of the Fish," *CW* 9ii, par. 170.
31. "Transformation Symbolism in the Mass," *Psychology and Religion, CW* 11, par. 390.
32. Ibid., par. 391.
33. Ibid., par. 390.
34. Ibid., par. 391.
35. Ibid., par. 398.
36. Ibid., par. 400.
37. Ibid., par. 390.

38. Ibid., par. 410.
39. Ibid., par. 445.
40. Ibid., par. 390.
41. Ibid., par. 419.
42. Ibid., par. 444.
43. Ibid.
44. Ibid., par. 446.
45. Ibid.
46. Ibid.: "In order to exorcise this danger, the Church has not made too much of the 'Christ within,' but has made all it possibly could of the Christ whom we 'have seen, heard, and touched with hands,' in other words, with the historical event 'below in Jerusalem.'"
47. Ibid.
48. Ibid.
49. Ibid., par. 443.
50. Ibid.
51. Ibid., pars. 553-758.
52. "A Psychological Approach to the Dogma of the Trinity," ibid., par. 254.
53. Ibid., par. 259.
54. "Christ, A Symbol of the Self," CW 9ii, par. 118.
55. "A Psychological Approach to the Trinity," CW 11, par. 260.
56. Ibid., par. 263.
57. Ibid.
58. Ibid., par. 267.
59. "The Spirit Mercurius," Alchemical Studies, CW 13, par. 295: "Hesitantly, as in a dream, the introspective brooding of the centuries gradually put together the figure of Mercurius and created a symbol which, according to all the psychological rules, stands in a compensatory relation to Christ."
60. Ibid., par. 252.
61. Ibid., par. 256.
62. Ibid.
63. Ibid., par. 289.
64. Letters II, p. 473.
65. "Paracelsus as a Spiritual Phenomenon," CW 13, par. 197.
66. ST II, p. 44.
67. Ibid.
68. Ibid., pp. 33-36.
69. Ibid., p. 61.
70. Ibid., p. 88.
71. Ibid., p. 94.
72. Ibid.
73. Ibid., p. 88.
74. Ibid., p. 98.
75. Ibid.

76.   Ibid., p. 109.
77.   Ibid., p. 114.
78.   Ibid.
79.   Ibid., p. 115.
80.   Ibid., p. 166.
81.   Ibid., p. 167.
82.   Ibid., p. 170.
83.   Ibid., p. 172.
84.   Ibid., p. 175.
85.   "A Psychological Approach to the Trinity," *CW* 11, par. 265.

5   Aspects of the Spirit
1.   "Spirit and Life," *The Structure and Dynamics of the Psyche, CW* 8, par. 602.
2.   "The Phenomenology of the Spirit in Fairytales," *The Archetypes and the Collective Unconscious, CW* 9i, par. 385.
3.   Ibid.
4.   Ibid.
5.   Ibid., par. 393.
6.   Ibid.
7.   "Spirit and Life," *CW* 8, par. 643.
8.   Ibid., par. 645: "One should, strictly speaking, describe this hypothetical consciousness simply as a 'wider' one, so as not to arouse the prejudice that it is necessarily higher in the intellectual or moral sense."
9.   Ibid: "It is this clear feeling of superiority that gives the phenomenon of the spirit its revelatory character and absolute authority—a dangerous quality, to be sure; for what we might perhaps call 'higher' consciousness is not always higher from the point of view of our conscious values and often contrasts violently with our accepted ideals."
10.   Ibid., par. 628.
11.   Ibid., par. 644.
12.   "The Psychological Foundations of Belief in Spirits," ibid., par. 587.
13.   Ibid., par. 590.
14.   Ibid: "The association of a collective content with the ego always produces a state of alienation, because something is added to the individual's consciousness which ought really to remain unconscious, that is, separated from the ego."
15.   Ibid., par. 597.
16.   "Spirit and Life," ibid., par. 645.
17.   "On the Nature of the Psyche," ibid., par. 425.
18.   Ibid.
19.   "The Phenomenology of the Spirit in Fairytales," *CW* 9i, par. 453.
20.   Ibid.
21.   Ibid., par. 454.
22.   Ibid., par. 455.
23.   "On the Nature of the Psyche," *CW* 8, par. 406.

24.   "On Psychic Energy," ibid., par. 98.
25.   "On the Nature of the Psyche," ibid., par. 408.
26.   Ibid., par. 414.
27.   Ibid., par. 415.
28.   "The Problem of Types in the History of Classical and Medieval Thought," *Psychological Types, CW* 6, par. 85.
29.   Ibid.
30.   Ibid.
31.   "On the Nature of the Psyche," *CW* 8, par. 413.
32.   *Mysterium Coniunctionis, CW* 14, par. 670.
33.   Ibid., par. 671.
34.   Ibid., par. 707.
35.   Ibid., par. 742.
36.   Ibid., par. 747.
37.   Ibid., par. 664.
38.   Ibid.
39.   Ibid., par. 662.
40.   Ibid., par. 760.
41.   "Transformation Symbolism in the Mass," *Psychology and Religion, CW* 11, par. 359.
42.   *ST* III, p. 11.
43.   Ibid., p. 15.
44.   Ibid., p. 125.
45.   Ibid., p. 114.
46.   Ibid., p. 112.
47.   Ibid., p. 127.
48.   Ibid., p. 231.
49.   Ibid.
50.   Ibid., p. 232.
51.   Ibid., pp. 233-234.
52.   Ibid., p. 235.
53.   Ibid., p. 237.
54.   Ibid., p. 272.

6   Church, Morality, and Eschatology
 1.   *Mysterium Coniunctionis, CW* 14, par. 520.
 2.   Ibid.
 3.   Ibid.
 4.   *ST* III, p. 116.
 5.   Ibid.
 6.   Ibid., p. 122.
 7.   Ibid.
 8.   Ibid., p. 123.

9. "The Permanent Significance of the Catholic Church for Protestants," *Dialog*, Vol. I (Summer, 1962), p. 23.

10. *ST* III, p. 121.

11. Ibid., p. 122

12. "A Psychological Approach to the Dogma of the Trinity," *Psychology and Religion, CW* 11, par. 285: "The situation in the Catholic camp is more subtle. Of especial importance here is the ritual with its sacral action, which dramatizes the living occurrence of archetypal meaning and thus makes a direct impact on the unconscious."

13. Ibid.

14. "Psychology and Religion," ibid., par. 82: "With the demolition of the protective walls, the Protestant lost the sacred images that expressed important unconscious factors, together with the ritual which, from time immemorial, has been a safe way of dealing with the unpredictable forces of the unconscious."

15. Ibid.

16. Ibid., par. 86: "If a Protestant survives the complete loss of his church and still remains a Protestant, that is to say a man who is defenceless against God and no longer shielded by walls or communities, he has a unique spiritual opportunity for immediate religious experience."

17. Ibid.: "The Protestant is left to God alone. For him there is no confession, no absolution, no possibility of an expiatory *opus divinum* of any kind. He has to digest his sins by himself; and, because the absence of a suitable ritual has put it beyond his reach, he is none too sure of divine grace."

18. Ibid.

19. "Answer to Job," ibid., par. 754.

20. *Mysterium Coniunctionis, CW* 14, par. 509.

21. *Letters* II, p. 77.

22. *ST* III, p. 274.

23. Ibid., p. 269.

24. Ibid., p. 274.

25. Ibid.

26. "Transformation Symbolism in the Mass," *CW* 11, par. 394: "The self cannot be equated either with collective morality or with natural instinct, but must be conceived as a determining factor whose nature is individual and unique. The superego is a necessary and unavoidable substitute for the experience of the self."

27. Ibid.

28. Ibid., par. 396.

29. *ST* III, pp. 399-400.

30. Ibid.

31. Ibid., pp. 400-401.

32. Ibid., p. 401.

33. Ibid., p. 405.

34. Ibid.

35. Ibid., p. 407.

36. Ibid., pp. 408-409.

37. Ibid.
38. Ibid., p. 416.
39. *Letters* II, pp. 133-138.
40. Ibid., p. 133: "Forget for once dogmatics and listen to what psychology has to say concerning your problem: *Christ as a symbol is far from being invalid,* although he is one side of the self and the devil the other."
41. Ibid., p. 135.
42. Ibid.
43. Ibid.
44. Ibid.
45. Ibid., p. 136.

Glossary of Jungian Terms

Anima (Latin, "soul"). The unconscious, feminine side of a man's personality. She is personified in dreams by images of women ranging from prostitute and seductress to spiritual guide (Wisdom). She is the Eros principle, hence a man's anima development is reflected in how he relates to women. Identification with the anima can appear as moodiness, effeminacy, and oversensitivity.

Animus (Latin, "spirit"). The unconscious, masculine side of a woman's personality. He personifies the Logos principle. Identification with the animus can cause a woman to become rigid, opinionated, and argumentative. More positively, he is the inner man who acts as a bridge between the woman's ego and her own creative resources in the unconscious.

Archetypes. Irrepresentable in themselves, but their effects appear in consciousness as the archetypal images and ideas. These are collective universal patterns or motifs which come from the collective unconscious and are the basic content of religions, mythologies, legends, and fairytales. They emerge in individuals through dreams and visions.

Association. A spontaneous flow of interconnected thoughts and images around a specific idea, determined by unconscious connections.

Complex. An emotionally charged group of ideas or images. At the "center" of a complex is an archetype or archetypal image.

Constellate. Whenever there is a strong emotional reaction to a person or a situation, a complex has been constellated (activated).

Ego. The central complex in the field of consciousness. A strong ego can relate objectively to activated contents of the unconscious (i.e., other complexes), rather than identifying with them, which appears as a state of possession.

Feeling. One of the four psychic functions. It is a rational function which evaluates the worth of relationships and situations. Feeling must be distinguished from emotion, which is due to an activated complex.

Individuation. The conscious realization of one's unique psychological reality, including both strengths and limitations. It leads to the experience of the Self as the regulating center of the psyche.

Inflation. A state in which one has an unrealistically high or low (negative inflation) sense of identity. It indicates a regression of consciousness into unconsciousness, which typically happens when the ego takes too many unconscious contents upon itself and loses the faculty of discrimination.

Intuition. One of the four psychic functions. It is the irrational function which tells us the possibilities inherent in the present. In contrast to sensation (the function which perceives immediate reality through the physical senses) intuition perceives via the unconscious, e.g., flashes of insight of unknown origin.

Participation mystique. A term derived from the anthropologist Lévy-Bruhl, denoting a primitive, psychological connection with objects, or between persons, resulting in a strong unconscious bond.

Persona (Latin, "actor's mask"). One's social role, derived from the expectations of society and early training. A strong ego relates to the outside world through a flexible persona; identification with a specific persona (doctor, scholar, artist, etc.) inhibits psychological development.

Projection. The process whereby an unconscious quality or characteristic of one's own is perceived and reacted to in an outer object or person. Projection of the anima or animus onto a real woman or man is experienced as falling in love. Frustrated expectations indicate the need to withdraw projections, in order to be able to relate to the reality of other people.

Puella aeternae (Latin, "eternal girl"). Indicates a certain type of woman who remains too long in adolescent psychology, generally associated with a strong unconscious attachment to the father. Her male counterpart is the **puer aeternus,** an "eternal youth" with a corresponding tie to the mother.

Self. The archetype of wholeness and the regulating center of the personality. It is experienced as a transpersonal power which transcends the ego, e.g., God.

Shadow. An unconscious part of the personality characterized by traits and attitudes which the conscious ego tends to reject. It is personified in dreams by persons of the same sex as the dreamer.

Symbol. The best possible expression for something essentially unknown. Symbolic thinking is non-linear, right-brain oriented; it is complementary to logical, linear, left-brain thinking.

Transcendent function. The reconciling "third" which emerges from the unconscious (in the form of a symbol or a new attitude) after the conflicting opposites have been consciously differentiated, and the tension between them held.

Transference and counter-transference. Particular cases of projection, commonly used to describe the unconscious, emotional bonds that arise between two persons in an analytic or therapeutic relationship.

Uroborus. The mythical snake or dragon that eats its own tail. It is a symbol both for individuation as a self-contained, circular process, and for narcissistic self-absorption.

Index

**CATALOGUE
AND ORDER FORM**

Studies in Jungian Psychology
by Jungian Analysts

LIMITED EDITION PAPERBACKS

Prices quoted are in U.S. dollars (except for Canadian orders)

1. The Secret Raven: Conflict and Transformation.
Daryl Sharp (Toronto). ISBN 0-919123-00-7. 128 pages. $10

A concise introduction to the application of Jungian psychology. Focuses on the creative personality—and the life and dreams of the writer Franz Kafka —but the psychology is relevant to anyone who has experienced a conflict between the spiritual life and sex, or between inner and outer reality. (Knowledge of Kafka is not necessary.) Illustrated. Bibliography.

2. The Psychological Meaning of Redemption Motifs in Fairytales.
Marie-Louise von Franz (Zurich). ISBN 0-919123-01-5. 128 pages. $10

A unique account of the significance of fairytales for an understanding of the process of individuation, especially in terms of integrating animal nature and human nature. Particularly helpful for its symbolic, nonlinear approach to the meaning of typical dream motifs (bathing, beating, clothes, animals, etc.), and its clear description of complexes and projection.

3. On Divination and Synchronicity: Psychology of Meaningful Chance.
Marie-Louise von Franz (Zurich). ISBN 0-919123-02-3. 128 pages. $10

A penetrating study of the meaning of the irrational. Examines time, number, and methods of divining fate such as the I Ching, astrology, Tarot, palmistry, random patterns, etc. Explains Jung's ideas on archetypes, projection, psychic energy and synchronicity, contrasting Western scientific attitudes with those of the Chinese and so-called primitives. Illustrated.

4. The Owl Was a Baker's Daughter: Obesity, Anorexia Nervosa, and the Repressed Feminine.
Marion Woodman (Toronto). ISBN 0-919123-03-1. 144 pages. $10

A pioneer work in feminine psychology, with particular attention to the body as mirror of the psyche in eating disorders and weight disturbances. Explores the personal and cultural loss—and potential rediscovery—of the feminine principle, through Jung's Association Experiment, case studies, dreams, Christianity and mythology. Illustrated. Glossary. Bibliography.

5. Alchemy: An Introduction to the Symbolism and the Psychology.
Marie-Louise von Franz (Zurich). ISBN 0-919123-04-X. 288 pages. $16

A lucid and practical guide to what the alchemists were really looking for— emotional balance and wholeness. Completely demystifies the subject. An important work, invaluable for an understanding of images and motifs in modern dreams and drawings, and indispensable for anyone interested in relationships and communication between the sexes. 84 Illustrations.

6. Descent to the Goddess: A Way of Initiation for Women.
Sylvia Brinton Perera (New York). ISBN 0-919123-05-8. 112 pages. $10

A timely and provocative study of women's freedom and the need for an inner, female authority in a masculine-oriented society. Based on the Sumerian goddess Inanna-Ishtar's journey to the underworld, her transformation through contact with her dark "sister" Ereshkigal, and her return. Rich in insights from dreams, mythology and analysis. Glossary. Bibliography.

7. **The Psyche as Sacrament: C.G. Jung and Paul Tillich.**
   John P. Dourley (Ottawa). ISBN 0-919123-06-6. 128 pages. $10

An illuminating, comparative study showing with great clarity that in the depths of the soul the psychological task and the religious task are one. With a dual perspective, the author—Jungian analyst and Catholic priest— examines the deeper meaning, for Christian and non-Christian alike, of God, Christ, the Spirit, the Trinity, morality and the religious life. Glossary.

8. **Border Crossings: Carlos Castaneda's Path of Knowledge.**
   Donald Lee Williams (Boulder). ISBN 0-919123-07-4. 160 pages. $12

The first thorough psychological examination of the popular don Juan novels. Using dreams, fairytales, and mythic and cultural parallels, the author brings Castaneda's spiritual journey down to earth, in terms of everyone's search for self-realization. Special attention to the psychology of women. (Familiarity with the novels is not necessary.) Glossary.

9. **Narcissism and Character Transformation: The Psychology of Narcissistic Character Disorders.**
   Nathan Schwartz-Salant (New York). ISBN 0-919123-08-2. 192 pp. $13

An incisive and comprehensive analysis of narcissism: what it looks like, what it means and how to deal with it. Shows how an understanding of the archetypal patterns that underlie the individual, clinical symptoms of narcissism can point the way to a healthy restructuring of the personality. Draws upon a variety of psychoanalytic points of view (Jungian, Freudian, Kohutian, Kleinian, etc.). Illustrated. Glossary. Bibliography.

10. **Rape and Ritual: A Psychological Study.**
    Bradley A. Te Paske (Minneapolis). ISBN 0-919123-09-0. 160 pp. $12

An absorbing combination of theory, clinical material, dreams and mythology, penetrating far beyond the actual deed to the impersonal, archetypal background of sexual assault. Special attention to male ambivalence toward women and the psychological significance of rape dreams and fantasies. Illustrated. Glossary. Bibliography.

11. **Alcoholism and Women: The Background and the Psychology.**
    Jan Bauer (Zurich). ISBN 0-919123-10-4. 144 pages. $12

A major contribution to an understanding of alcoholism, particularly in women. Compares and contrasts medical and psychological models, illustrates the relative merits of Alcoholics Anonymous and individual therapy, and presents new ways of looking at the problem based on case material, dreams and archetypal patterns. Glossary. Bibliography.

12. **Addiction to Perfection: The Still Unravished Bride.**
    Marion Woodman (Toronto). ISBN 0-919123-11-2. 208 pages. $12

A powerful and authoritative look at the psychology and attitudes of modern woman, expanding on the themes introduced in *The Owl Was a Baker's Daughter*. Explores the nature of the feminine through case material, dreams and mythology, in food rituals, rape symbolism, perfectionism, imagery in the body, sexuality and creativity. Illustrated.

13. **Jungian Dream Interpretation: A Handbook of Theory and Practice.**
    James A. Hall, M.D. (Dallas). ISBN 0-919123-12-0. 128 pages. $12

A comprehensive and practical guide to an understanding of dreams in light of the basic concepts of Jungian psychology. Jung's model of the psyche is described and discussed, with many clinical examples. Particular attention to common dream motifs, and how dreams are related to the stage of life and individuation process of the dreamer. Glossary.

14. **The Creation of Consciousness: Jung's Myth for Modern Man.**
Edward F. Edinger, M.D. (Los Angeles). ISBN 0-919123-13-9. 128 pages. $12

An important new book by the author of *Ego and Archetype,* proposing a new world-view based on a creative collaboration between the scientific pursuit of knowledge and the religious search for meaning. Explores the significance for mankind of Jung's life and work; discusses the purpose of human life and what it means to be conscious; examines the theological and psychological implications of Jung's master-work, *Answer to Job;* presents a radical, psychological understanding of God's "continuing incarnation"; and illustrates the pressing need for man to become more conscious of his dark, destructive side as well as his creative potential. Illustrated.

15. **The Analytic Encounter: Transference and Human Relationship.**
Mario Jacoby (Zurich). ISBN 0-919123-14-7. 128 pages. $12

A sensitive and revealing study that differentiates relationships based on projection from those characterized by psychological distance and mutual respect. Examines the psychodynamics activated in any intimate relationship, and particularly in therapy and analysis; summarizes the views of Jung and Freud on identification, projection and transference-countertransference, as well as those of Martin Buber (I-It and I-Thou relationships); and shows how unconscious complexes may appear in dreams and emotional reactions. Special attention to the so-called narcissistic transferences (mirror, idealizing, etc.), the archetypal roots of projection and the significance of erotic love in the analytic situation. Glossary. Bibliography.

16. **Change of Life: A Psychological Study of the Menopause.**
Ann Mankowitz (Santa Fe). ISBN 0-919123-15-5. 128 pages. $12

A detailed and profoundly moving account of a menopausal woman's Jungian analysis, openly facing the fears and apprehensions behind the collective "conspiracy of silence" that surrounds this crucial period of every woman's life. Dramatically interweaves the experience of one woman with more generally applicable social, biological, emotional and psychological factors; frankly discusses the realities of aging, within which the menopause is seen as a potentially creative rite of passage; and illustrates how the menopause may manifest, both in outer life and in dreams, as a time of rebirth, an opportunity for psychological integration and growth, increased strength and wisdom. Glossary. Bibliography.

All books contain detailed Index

INNER CITY BOOKS
Box 1271, Station Q, Toronto, Canada M4T 2P4
(416) 927-0355

ORDER FORM

Please detach and fill out both sides
*Prices quoted are in U.S. dollars
(except for Canadian orders)*

Title	Price	Copies	Amount
1. Raven	$10	_____	_____
2. Redemption	$10	_____	_____
3. Divination	$10	_____	_____
4. The Owl	$10	_____	_____
5. Alchemy	$16	_____	_____
6. Descent	$10	_____	_____
7. Psyche	$10	_____	_____
8. Border	$12	_____	_____
9. Narcissism	$13	_____	_____
10. Rape	$12	_____	_____
11. Alcoholism	$12	_____	_____
12. Addiction	$12	_____	_____
13. Dream	$12	_____	_____
14. Creation	$12	_____	_____
15. Encounter	$12	_____	_____
16. Change	$12	_____	_____

Subtotal: _____

Less Discount if applicable: _____

Or Plus Postage/Handling (80¢ per book): _____

TOTAL: _____

Orders from outside Canada pay in $U.S.

Make check or money order payable to **INNER CITY BOOKS**

REMARKS

INNER CITY BOOKS
Box 1271, Station Q
Toronto, Canada M4T 2P4

(See reverse for Order Form)

Cheque or Money Order enclosed for: _____

Please send books to:

NAME: _____

ADDRESS: _____

_____ Zip or Postal Code: _____

Please send _____ Catalogues and Order Forms to me _____ and/or:

NAME: _____

ADDRESS: _____

_____ Zip or Postal Code: _____

Please send Catalogues to my local Bookseller:

_____

_____

_____